Dreamweaver MX 2004
Right from the Start

By F.R. Heathcote

Published by

PAYNE-GALLWAY
PUBLISHERS LTD

26–28 Northgate Street, Ipswich IP1 3DB
Tel: 01473 251097 • Fax: 01473 232758

www.payne-gallway.co.uk

Acknowledgements

Thank you to my partner Simon who made the time to work through my first draft, but sadly did not live to see it in print.

Thanks go to Purple Ski (www.purpleski.com) for the use of their lovely chalet photos used throughout this book.

Published by Payne-Gallway Publishers Ltd
An imprint of Harcourt Education Ltd
Halley Court, Jordan Hill,Oxford. OX2 8EJ

First Edition 2004

Cover illustration © Richard Chasemore 2003
Cover Design © Direction Advertising & Design Ltd.

© F.R. Heathcote 2004
10 09 08 07 06
10 9 8 7 6 5 4

10-digit ISBN: 1 904467 80 6

13-digit ISBN: 978 1 904467 80 9

Printed and bound in China by China Translation & Printing Services Ltd.

Contents

What is Dreamweaver?

Dreamweaver is a web authoring tool used to create web pages. As you may or may not know, the code used to write web pages is called HTML (HyperText Markup Language). Before the days of packages such as Dreamweaver, people used to create web pages purely by writing HTML code – if you wanted a particular image to appear on a page, you couldn't just insert the image in the right place, you had to write the code to position it and to retrieve the correct image file. You'll be relieved to hear that with Dreamweaver, all you do is insert the image wherever you want on a page – in about three mouse clicks.

Web pages are still coded in HTML, but you don't even have to know it exists, because you just tell Dreamweaver in simple terms how you want the web page to look, and it writes all the HTML for you! Dreamweaver is called a WYSIWYG program, short for What You See is What You Get, for the simple reason that Dreamweaver always shows you an accurate picture of what the final web page will look like. It is advisable as you become more familiar with Dreamweaver to learn how HTML works (this is mainly useful for debugging, if for some reason Dreamweaver doesn't do what you want it to), but to begin with you can get away with ignoring it completely.

> **Tip:** A **website** is a collection of **web pages**, linked together by a menu system. In this book you will build a complete website by creating the web pages individually and then linking them together.

Getting Dreamweaver

If you don't already have Dreamweaver installed, you can purchase a copy from their website www.dreamweaver.com, or alternatively download a free fully working 30-day trial version. Full instructions on how to buy or trial the package are on the website.

Additional Software

Dreamweaver is produced by Macromedia who produce several other software programs for web developers such as Flash and Fireworks. This book does not assume you have any of these additional programs.

It is nice when developing web pages to be able to create your own simple graphics, if only to create smart-looking buttons and menus. You don't need a graphics package to work through this book because you can download all the graphics used from the Payne-Gallway website (you'll be talked through this later). If you do want to have a go at designing your own graphics, two of the simplest and cheapest graphics packages are Photoshop Elements and Paint Shop Pro; the latter was used to create the graphics you'll download later.

> **Tip:** If you want to learn more about Photoshop Elements or Paint Shop Pro, look at **Photoshop Elements Right from the Start** or **Basic Paint Shop Pro** both by R. Chasemore – visit **www.payne-gallway.co.uk** for details.

The Alpe Retreats website

Throughout this book you will create and develop a website for a company called Alpe Retreats. Alpe Retreats is a small company that owns and runs four chalets in Val Thorens in the French Alps. They need a website so that anyone looking for a chalet in Val Thorens can look up the details and prices. They would also like customers to be able to view the availability of the chalets and fill in a provisional booking form on the website that is then e-mailed to the company.

The first step when creating any web page is to get a good picture in your mind of what you want the website to look like and what it needs to contain. You should plan it out on paper before jumping onto the computer.

A rough plan of the pages that will make up the Alpe Retreats website is shown on the next two pages. There are six links on the left of each page that, when clicked, will take the user to the relevant page. Notice that the menu (also called a navigation bar) and the title are the same on every page.

HOME PAGE — general info about
Alpe Retreats + photo
of a chalet.

RESORT PAGE — general info about
Val Thorens.

A second chalets menu appears
when cursor is on CHALETS link.
User can click on chalet name
to view chalet details.

ALPE RETREATS

HOME
RESORT
CHALETS
PRICES
BOOKING
CONTACT

CHALETS > chalet 3

CHALETS > chalet 3 PAGE — info and photo of chalet.

ALPE RETREATS

HOME
RESORT
CHALETS
PRICES
BOOKING
CONTACT

PRICES

Date	Chalet 1	Chalet 2	...
—	—	—	
⋮	⋮	⋮	

PRICES PAGE — list of dates + prices for all chalets

ALPE RETREATS

HOME
RESORT
CHALETS
PRICES
BOOKING
CONTACT

BOOKING

Name
Address

Date
Chalet
⋮   ⋮   SUBMIT

BOOKING PAGE — user will fill out a booking form which is then emailed to Alpe Retreats.

ALPE RETREATS

HOME
RESORT
CHALETS
PRICES
BOOKING
CONTACT

CONTACT

Address

Phone
email   —@—

Creating a New Website

2

In this chapter we will create the Alpe Retreats website. You'll learn how to define a site and set up a good file structure for the whole site.

◉ Load Dreamweaver. You can do this in one of two ways:

◉ *Either* double-click the Dreamweaver icon on your windows desktop

◉ *Or* click Start, Programs then find the Macromedia folder and select Dreamweaver.

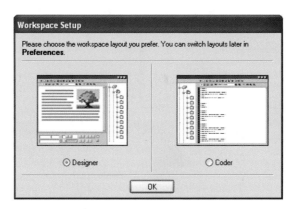

Figure 2.1: The Workspace Setup window

Note: In version MX choose Dreamweaver MX workspace.

◉ Choose Designer by making sure the first option button is selected, then click OK.

You will then see this window (MX 2004 only):

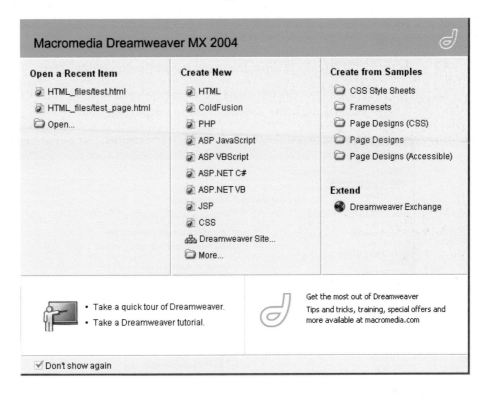

Figure 2.2: The Start Page appears if this is the first time you've opened
Dreamweaver MX 2004

Tip: The start page does not appear in Dreamweaver MX, only MX 2004.

You don't want to see this Start Page screen every time you open Dreamweaver, so click
the box in the bottom-left of the screen marked **Don't show again**. Click **OK** in the
dialogue box that appears.

Figure 2.3

The green Start Page will stay open until we choose an option from it.

Changing workspace options

If you selected the wrong workspace option you can correct it using the Preferences window as shown below.

◉   Select Edit, Preferences from the menu bar at the top of the screen.

◉   Select General from the left-hand list of categories then click the Change Workspace button. This will open the window shown in Figure 2.1 above.

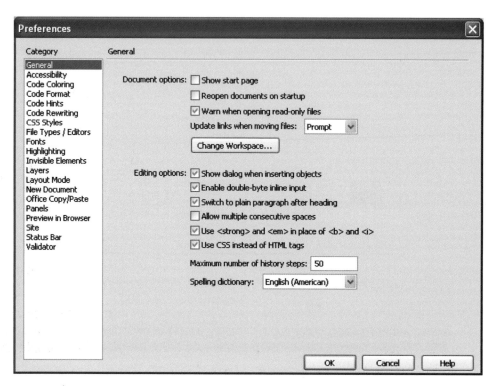

Figure 2.4: Preferences

◉   Click OK to close the Preferences window.

Folder structure

When you set up a new site, you will be asked where on your computer you want it to be saved. It is therefore a good idea to create a suitable folder structure before opening a new site.

Each page on your site and each image you use will be a separate file. By the time you've created a website with many pages and images there will be a lot of files, so you need to make sure they are well-organised from the start.

For any website, the main folders you will want are:

HTML files

Each page in your website will be an HTML file, and will go in this folder.

Images

Any image inserted on a web page is stored separately as an image file, and should be put in this folder. The image files used in the Alpe Retreats website are all JPEG (.jpg) files; other common file types used for images are .gif and .png.

Library

The library is not actually used in this book but we'll create the folder anyway because it is good practice.

When you are creating your website, you can add various objects such as images or paragraphs of text to the library. This is useful for items that are used often, because if a library item is updated, every instance of this library item is also updated. Each item added to the library is given its own library file, which is stored in this folder.

Templates

As soon as you create a template, Dreamweaver will automatically create the Templates folder for you, so you won't need to create that. You can create templates in Dreamweaver in much the same way as Word. Once the template is created, you can base subsequent pages on that template. All template files have the file extension .dwt and will be stored in this folder.

Creating the folders

You can create the folders using the Files panel in Dreamweaver. However, if you are completely new to Dreamweaver it may be advisable to use Windows Explorer because you will be more familiar with it. We'll use the Files panel later.

Using Windows Explorer

To create the folders in Windows Explorer.

○   Open Windows Explorer by right-clicking on the Start button and clicking Explore from the context menu that appears.

Figure 2.5: Opening Windows Explorer from the Start Menu

○   Find a suitable place to put the website folders; this will probably be somewhere in My Documents.

○   Create a folder and name it Alpe Retreats Website.

○   Create three more folders in the Alpe Retreats Website folder named HTML_files, Images and Library. You don't need to create the Templates folder yet because Dreamweaver will create it for you when you save your first template.

Your file structure should now look like this:

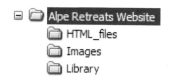

Figure 2.6: The file structure

○   Close Explorer and return to Dreamweaver.

Using the Files panel

◉   In Dreamweaver, click the Files panel in the Files panel group.

Tip: In version MX the **Files** panel is called the **Site** panel.

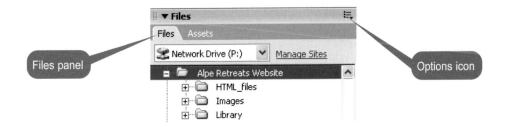

Figure 2.7: The Files panel in the Files panel group

 ◉   If you have already created your folders, you should be able to navigate to them in just the same way you would in Explorer. If you haven't created them yet, click the options icon at the top right of the Files panel then select File from the menu. Here you can select to create a new folder.

Creating a new site

◉   If the green Start Page is still visible, select the Dreamweaver Site... option in the centre column marked Create New.

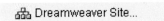

◉   If the Start Page is not visible, select Site, Manage Sites... from the main menu bar.

Figure 2.8: The Site menu

Note: Select **New Site** from the **Site** menu in version MX.

◉   In the Manage Sites window click the New button, then click Site on the small sub-menu that appears.

The Site Definition window appears. By default the Basic tab will be selected. This will take you through the Wizard. We will not use the wizard, as it includes a lot of options that we just don't need at this stage.

○ Click the Advanced tab.

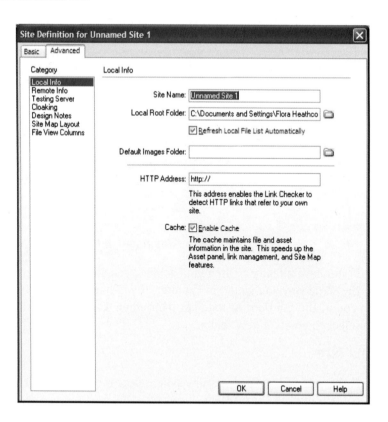

Figure 2.9: Site Definition

○ Enter Alpe Retreats as the name for the website.

 ○ Click the Browse icon next to the Local Root Folder field and locate the folder Alpe Retreats Website you just created.

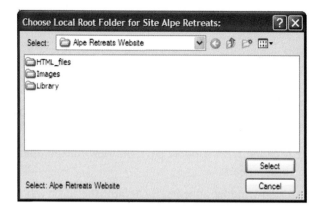

Figure 2.10: Selecting a local root folder for the site

◑ Click Select.

◑ You don't need to fill in any of the other options just yet, so just click OK, then click Done in the Manage Sites window.

❶ If you want to change any of the options you've just set, go to Site, Manage Sites... on the main menu bar. Select the Alpe Retreats site and click the Edit button.

All done! You've set up the Alpe Retreats site.

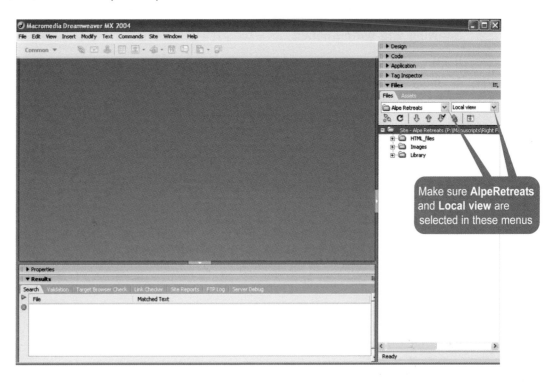

Figure 2.11: The Dreamweaver MX 2004 workspace

Tip: In version MX, the workspace will open with a new blank page called **Untitled-1** already created. You can leave this open for now.

Your screen should now look like the one above. Rather than introducing all the different parts of the workspace now, we'll just cover a few basics here and then the rest as you need them.

Panels

Many of the useful commands in Dreamweaver are contained in panels. Panels are very similar to windows which you will have come across in other applications. They can be hidden, minimised or closed in a similar way to windows. The panels are located to the right of the workspace – there are about five panel groups in that list (Design, Code, Application, Tag Inspector and Files). Don't worry – you don't need to know about most of these right now, in fact in this book you'll only need to use about half of them.

Showing and hiding panels

If you are missing any of the panels shown in Figure 2.11, follow the steps below to add them to your workspace. You don't need to do this now – you can wait until you need to use a particular panel if you like.

● Select Window from the main menu bar.

❶ Some of the panels are grouped, for example the Files panel (Site panel in version MX) and the Assets panel are both in the Files panel group. If you open one of the panels in a group, the whole group will open.

● Only the names of the panels appear in the Window menu – not the panel groups. To open a panel click the name of the panel in the Window menu. It should then appear on the right of the screen with the other panels.

 ● To close a panel group, click the options icon in the top right of the panel group, and select Close Panel Group from the menu.

Window	
✔ Insert	Ctrl+F2
Properties	Ctrl+F3
✔ CSS Styles	Shift+F11
Layers	F2
Behaviors	Shift+F3
Snippets	Shift+F9
Reference	Shift+F1
Databases	Ctrl+Shift+F10
Bindings	Ctrl+F10
Server Behaviors	Ctrl+F9
Components	Ctrl+F7
✔ Files	F8
Assets	F11
Tag Inspector	F9
Results	F7
History	Shift+F10
Frames	Shift+F2
Code Inspector	F10
Arrange Panels	
Hide Panels	F4
Cascade	
Tile Horizontally	
Tile Vertically	
Untitled-1	

Figure 2.12:
The Window menu

Expanding and collapsing panel groups

The panel groups are designed so that you can expand and collapse them, depending on which one you are using at the time. In Figure 2.11 the Files panel group is expanded.

◉ To expand or collapse a panel, just click the small arrow next to the panel name.

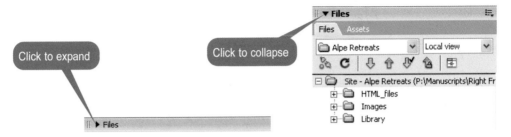

Figure 2.13: Expanding & collapsing a panel

Resizing panels

You can resize the width of the panels by clicking and dragging the grey border between the panel groups and the page.

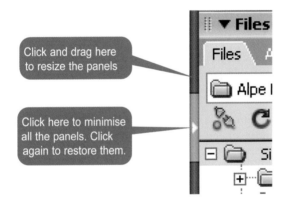

Figure 2.14: Widening panels

The Files panel

Notice that all the folders you have set up now appear in the Files panel. Dreamweaver has inserted the text Site – Alpe Retreats where the folder name Alpe Retreats Website was (this is because Alpe Retreats was the name you gave to the site when setting up); the file pathname next to the text gives the original folder name.

If your folders don't appear in the Files panel, make sure you have Alpe Retreats and Local View selected as shown below:

Figure 2.15

You can easily change folder names, add new folders or delete files using the Files panel – you don't need to use Windows Explorer. All folders that are associated with a website are coloured green; because you specified that the site would be stored in the Alpe Retreats Website folder, all folders within that folder will be associated with that website and will be coloured green.

Creating and saving a web page

All the pages you create for the Alpe Retreats website will be based on a template that we will create in the next chapter. Here we'll create and save a web page that is not based on a template, just for practice. We'll then delete the page.

First we need to create a new blank page if you don't already have one open (in version MX there may already be a blank page called Untitled-1 already created).

◉   Select File, New from the main menu bar.

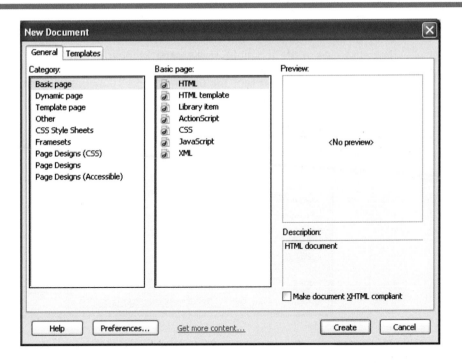

Figure 2.16: Creating a basic HTML page

⊙   Leave the options as **Basic page** and **HTML** and click **Create**.

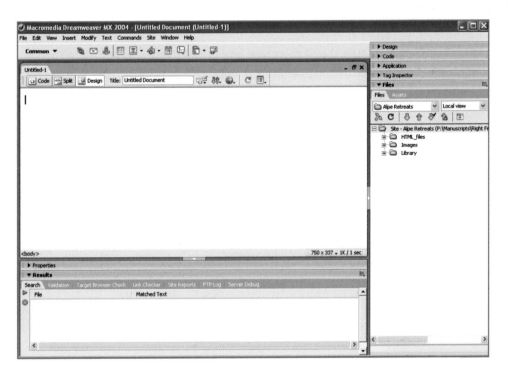

Figure 2.17: A blank page is created

○ If the Untitled-1 page doesn't take up the whole window as shown above, click the Maximise icon at the top-right of the page window.

○ From the main menu bar (not the one in the Files panel), select File, Save As.

The Save As dialogue box appears.

○ We'll save it in the HTML_files folder, so double-click this. Now enter the file name test_page.html in the File name box.

Figure 2.18: Saving a web page

Tip: If you don't add the file extension **.html** after the file name, the files will be automatically saved with a **.htm** extension instead. These two file types are exactly the same, but some servers don't like the use of **.htm** files. It is therefore safer to save all files as **.html** files because all servers can work with these.

○ Notice that in the Save as type box it lists many different file extensions next to All Documents, not just one; this is fine. Click Save when your screen looks like the one above.

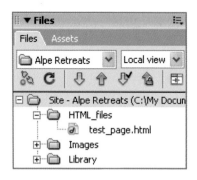

The page appears as an HTML file in the Files panel

Figure 2.19

○ In the Files panel, click the small plus symbol next to the HTML_files folder. You should now be able to see the test_page file. Notice that it has saved the file with a .html file extension.

The test_page file now represents one web page within your website – although it is currently blank.

Deleting a web page

To delete a web page, all you do is delete its file. To avoid confusing error messages, it is best to make sure a file is closed before you try and delete it.

Closing a page

◉ Close the test_page by right-clicking on the page tab and selecting Close from the context menu that appears.

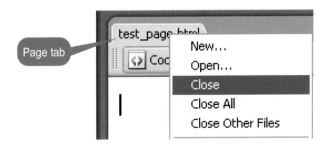

Figure 2.20: Closing a page

Tip: In version MX the page tab will be at the bottom of the page, not the top.

The page will disappear.

❶ If you wanted to open the page again, you would just double-click it in the Files panel.

◉ In the Files panel, click to select the test_page file. Now press the Delete key.

Figure 2.21: Deleting a page

◉ Click Yes (or OK in version MX).

❶ If you try to delete a page without closing it first, it will still remain open, and you will see messages saying you should resave it, and asking if you want to. If this happens, don't resave.

Deleting pages that are linked to other pages

If you try and delete a page that has links to it from another page, Dreamweaver will list the links to the site and ask for confirmation that you wish to delete the page.

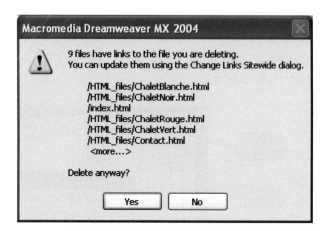

Figure 2.22: Deleting a linked page

◉   If you just agree to Dreamweaver's warnings it will delete the page OK. If you get a message about links, this means that when you delete the page, another page will contain a link that doesn't do anything! Open up the page(s) that Dreamweaver says contains the link and delete the link.

Help

The Dreamweaver help functions are on the Help menu.

> **Tip:** For help in version MX see the **Answers** panel. If you can't see the **Answers** panel select **Window**, **Answers** from the main menu bar.

❶   If you need any extra help with anything select Help, Getting Started and Tutorials from the main menu bar. From here you have access to the Tutorials, as well as Help Contents, Search and Index.

❶   If you need help on a particular subject, click the Search tab and enter the subject in the space at the top of the window. Click List Topics to see what help is available. Alternatively you can search the Help Index by clicking the Index tab.

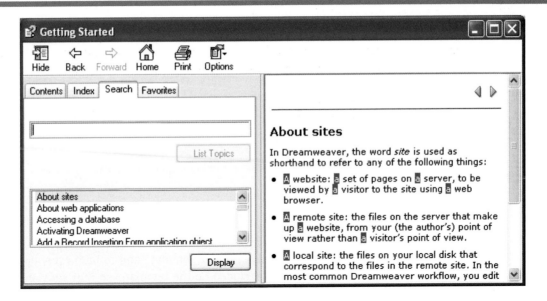

Figure 2.23: Getting help

 When you have finished using the help functions, click the red Close icon.

Creating a Template 3

You'll be pleased to hear that this is where the fun, creative bit starts. The key to a really professional-looking website is to use a clean, simple template and to base every page on the same template. The navigation bar is also included on the template, so that whichever page you are on you have access to the same navigation buttons. This not only makes the website look professional and coherent, it also makes it easy for people to browse your website without getting lost!

You can have a lot of fun creating your own buttons and logos to use on this website using a simple graphics package. However, if you don't want to learn a graphics package or you just don't have the time, the first thing you need to do is download all the images used in advance – if you download everything now, you'll have all the necessary images to hand for the rest of the book.

Downloading the image files

All the image files you need to create the Alpe Retreats website can be downloaded from the Payne-Gallway website. Go to www.payne-gallway.co.uk/dreamweaver and follow the onscreen instructions.

Make sure you download the images into the Images folder that you set up in the last chapter. When you have downloaded them all, your file structure should look like Figure 3.1 in the Files panel.

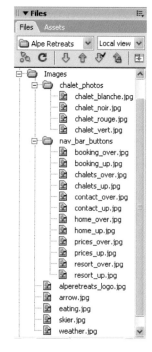

Figure 3.1: The Files panel after downloading the image files

Creating a new template

You can create a template from scratch or an existing page can be converted into a template. We'll create a basic page and then later save it as a template.

◉ Select File, New from the main menu bar.

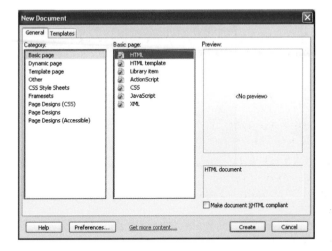

Figure 3.2: The New Document window

Tip: You could create a template page by selecting **HTML Template** from the **Basic Page** list. This would achieve the same result as saving the basic page as a template.

◉ Make sure Basic Page is selected in the Category list and HTML from the second list. Click Create.

Figure 3.3: The new blank page appears

Saving a page as a template

Remember – you've opened a new page, but it is not yet saved. When a file is saved it will appear in the Files panel. We'll save the page now as a template.

◉   Select File, Save as Template... from the main menu bar.

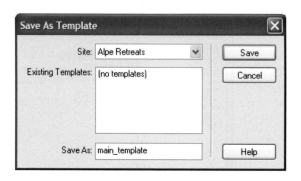

Figure 3.4: Saving a page as a template

◉   Save the template as main_template and click Save.

The template may not yet be shown in the Files panel – you will need to refresh it first.

◉   In the Files panel, click the Refresh icon.

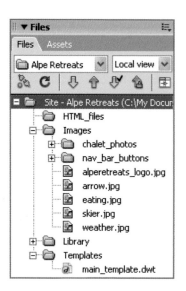

Figure 3.5: The main_template file appears in the Files panel

ⓘ   Although you didn't specify where Dreamweaver should save the file, it has automatically created a Templates folder and put it in there. If you had created the Templates folder along with the others, it would have found that and saved it in there.

Tables

You've probably come across tables in Microsoft Word, where they are used to store data in columns and rows. Well, in Dreamweaver tables can be used to store columns and rows of data, but their main use is actually as a layout tool.

By using a large table, the size of the whole web page, you can adjust the columns and rows to divide up the page into sections.

A large table, the width of the whole page, will be the basis of our template.

The Insert bar

Whenever you want to insert anything, whether it be a table, an image, a nav bar etc, you will use the Insert bar. This is located at the top of the screen, just below the main menu bar.

There are two different views of the Insert bar. The one which appears when you first open Dreamweaver is the one above; we will now change this to show tabs.

⦿   Click where it says Common on the Insert bar, then select Show as Tabs from the menu that appears.

The insert bar now appears as shown below:

    Tip: To revert to the original view, click the small menu icon in the top right of the **Insert** bar and select **Show as Menu** from the list.

We'll leave the Insert bar looking like this.

🛈   If you want to know what any of the icons are on the Insert bar, just hold the mouse over the icon for a few seconds, and the Tool tip will appear with the name of the icon.

Inserting a table

○ Make sure the cursor is in the top left of the page (it will be unless you've moved it), this is where we want to insert the table.

○ Click the Table icon on the Insert bar (it is under the Common tab, which should already be selected).

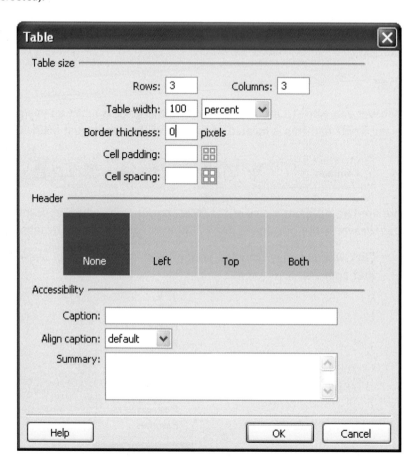

Figure 3.6: The Insert Table window

Tip: You can just enter a width in pixels if you know the size you want. Most sites use a width of about **800** pixels. At this size, each page of your site will fit onto most screens without users having to scroll across. Some sites are as narrow as **600** pixels – this means that even people with relatively small screens can view a page without scrolling, but you can't fit as much on a page. **www.payne-gallway.co.uk** uses a width of 600 pixels. **www.bbc.co.uk** uses just less than **800**.

▶ Fill out the Table dialogue box as above, with 3 rows and 3 columns. Enter the width as 100%. A value of 0 for the border gives an invisible border.

❶ In Dreamweaver you can choose whether to size an object in relative or absolute terms. You can size an object relative to the size of the browser window by giving the size as a percentage. You can give an absolute size by specifying the number of pixels. It's difficult to gauge the size you want a table in pixels, so it is often easier to create a table as 100%, resize it by eye, then convert all lengths to pixels. By specifying the sizes in pixels you can more easily cater for people with smaller screen sizes. We'll leave the sizes as percent for now and look at how to change them to pixels later.

▶ Click OK.

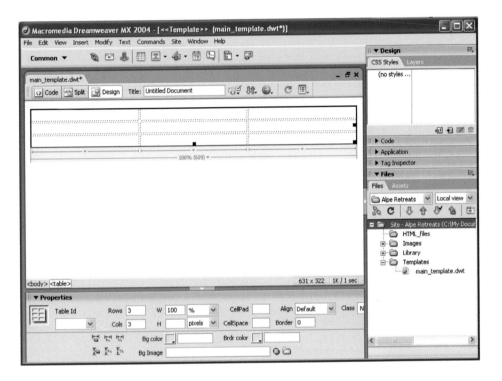

Figure 3.7: The new table appears at the top of the page

The table appears as shown above. It will need resizing but we'll do that in a minute.

Selecting cells, rows and tables

The table in the screenshot above is selected – as yours probably is because you've just created it. You can tell that it is selected because it has a solid black border and small black handles around it. It also has green lines and text indicating the width of the table.

○ Click away from the table to deselect it. The handles and green lines will disappear.

○ Now click in the middle of the table. Look at the text at the bottom left of the page:

These are called tags, and the area they are in is called the Tag selector. Clicking on them here will select the objects they represent.

Clicking <td> will select the cell that the cursor is in.

Clicking <tr> will select the row the cursor is in.

Clicking <table> will select the table the cursor is in.

○ Click each of these tags in turn and watch the black border highlight different parts of the table. This is the easiest way to select parts of a table.

The Properties inspector

At the bottom of the screen is the Properties inspector (it is essentially another panel, but Dreamweaver calls it an inspector not a panel). You can immediately view the properties of any object on the page just by selecting it.

 If you can't see the Properties inspector, select Window, Properties from the main menu bar. If the panel is collapsed, just click the small black arrow to the left of where it says Properties.

◐ Select the table you've just created by clicking the <table> tag.

Figure 3.8: The Properties inspector

❶ If your Properties inspector is smaller than the one above you might need to expand yours. To do this, just click the small arrow in the bottom right of the Properties inspector.

The table properties appear in the Properties inspector. You'll learn more about these properties in a minute.

◐ Look at the properties of a cell and row by selecting them and viewing them in the Properties inspector.

Inserting and deleting rows and columns

Adding or deleting the last row or column

You can add or delete the bottom row or right-hand column simply by changing the number of rows and columns in the table properties (in the Properties inspector).

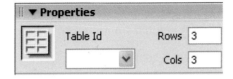

◐ Make sure the table is selected. Change the number of rows to 4 and columns to 2 using the Properties inspector.

> **Tip:** When changing properties in the **Properties** inspector, you need to either tab out of a cell or press **Return** for the changes to take effect.

❶ Another way to add a row is to place the cursor in the last cell in a table and press the Tab key.

Inserting or deleting a row or column in the middle of a table

❍ Right-click in the top left cell in the table.

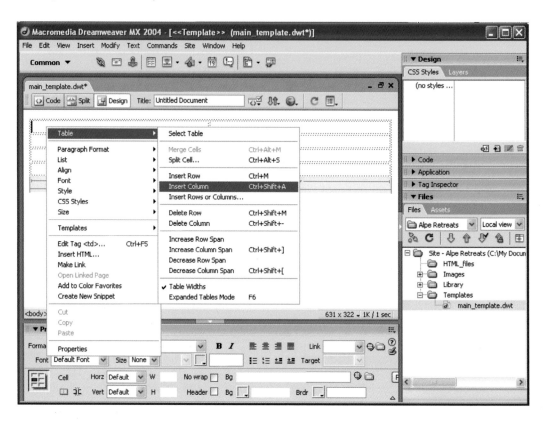

Figure 3.9: Inserting a column

❍ Select Table, Insert Column from the context menu that appears.

The table should now have 3 columns.

❍ Use the same method to delete one of the rows.

Merging and splitting cells

You can easily merge and split cells, so that the number of rows and columns varies across the table. The quickest way to merge and split cells is to use the icons in the Properties inspector.

Merging

 ◉ Select the entire second row in the table. Click the Merge Cells icon in the Properties inspector.

Figure 3.10: Merging cells

The cells are merged, and there's only one column in the second row.

Splitting

◉ Select the centre cell in row 3.

 ◉ Click the Split Cells icon in the Properties inspector.

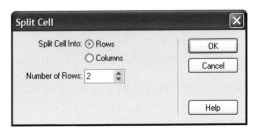

Figure 3.11: Splitting cells

The Split Cell dialogue box appears. You have the choice of splitting the cell into rows or columns. You can also specify how many rows or columns.

◉ Enter the settings shown above, and then click OK.

Figure 3.12: Splitting cells

The cell is split in two horizontally.

Resizing cells and tables

Resizing a table

The table should at least fill the visible area on the screen, so we need to make it much longer.

◉   Select the whole table. Place the mouse over the bottom handle so that it becomes a small double-headed arrow.

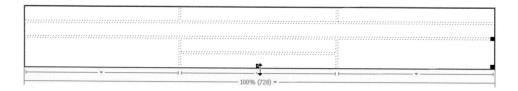

Figure 3.13: Resizing a table

◉   Click and drag the handle down so that the table is about **1000** pixels (the height will be shown in the **Properties** inspector). Release the mouse when you're happy with the size.

> **Tip:** You don't need to worry that a table cell won't be big enough to fit an object because the table will always grow to fit whatever you put in.

Resizing cells

To resize cells, just click and drag the table border between the cells.

◉   Place the mouse over the border you want to resize so that the cursor becomes an arrow.

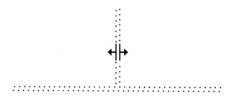

◉   Click and drag the border to where you want it, then release it.

◉   Click and drag the borders so that your table looks like Figure 3.14. First try and get the relative sizes of the cells correct – you will probably find that the total height of the table changes when you do this. If so, just select the table then click and drag the bottom border to resize the height to about 1000 pixels. I'm afraid resizing tables isn't an exact science in Dreamweaver; it sometimes takes a bit of trial and error – and a lot of patience!

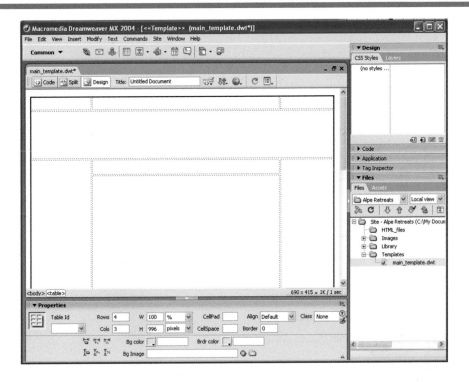

Figure 3.14

Converting the table widths to pixels

Now that the table is the right size, we'll convert the widths from % to pixels. Percentages are good if you want the template to resize according to how large a browser window is, but because people will be viewing your website on different sized screens it is best to size the table for a fairly average screen size in absolute measurements. The other problem when the page resizes to fit the browser window is that the layout can change, so your designs might be messed up.

- Select the whole table by clicking the <table> tag at the bottom of the page.

 - Click the Convert Table Widths to Pixels icon at the bottom of the Properties inspector. The width should be about 800 pixels.

Now click the Convert Table Heights to Pixels icon. The height may have already been displayed in pixels in which case nothing will have changed. The height should be about 1000 pixels.

You can type in exact values for the width and height in the Properties inspector.

 Tip: You can change the table widths and heights back to **%** at any time by clicking the **Convert Widths/Heights to Percent** icons (next to the **Convert Widths/Heights to Pixels** icons).

Saving the template

It's important to save your work regularly. You save a template in just the same way as you would a normal page.

Make sure the main_template page tab is selected at the top of the screen (it should be the only page open).

Select File, Save from the main menu bar.

You'll see a message about editable regions – we'll create these later. Just click OK.

When saving a template that you have based another page on you will get the following message. Don't worry – just click Yes and Dreamweaver will do all the hard work and update all the relevant pages for you. Click Close in the Update Pages dialogue box when it has finished updating.

Figure 3.15

Tip: If the **Save** option is greyed-out on the menu this is because the template is already saved. If this is the case, just go on to the next step.

Inserting Images

Now we'll start inserting images in the various sections of the table. For this we'll use the Insert Image icon on the Insert bar.

○ Place the cursor in the second row. Click the down-arrow to display the drop-down list next to the 5th icon along on the Insert bar. Select Image from the list.

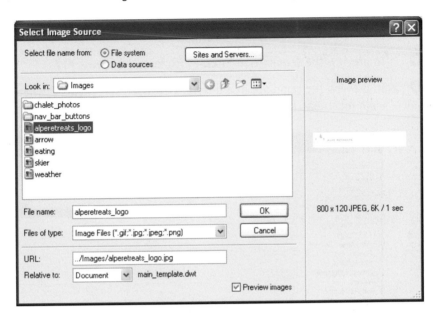

Figure 3.16: Locating the image file

○ The image you want is in the Images folder. Click to select alperetreats_logo.jpg then click OK.

The image appears in the second row.

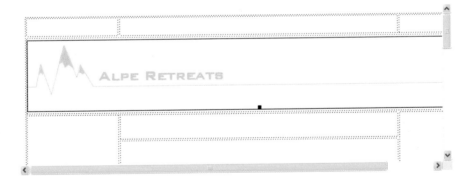

Figure 3.17: The image appears where the cursor was

Previewing the template

It's very easy to see what the template will look like when viewed in a browser.

- ▶ Before previewing any page or template you should save it first. If you don't save, the latest changes might not be shown in the browser. Select File, Save from the menu. Click OK to the message about editable regions.

- ▶ You might get a message about updating other documents based on the template – you don't have any pages based on this template yet so just click No.

- ▶ To preview the template in Internet Explorer, just press F12.

- ▶ To preview the template in a different browser, select File, Preview in Browser from the main menu bar. If the browser you want isn't listed, select Edit Browser List...

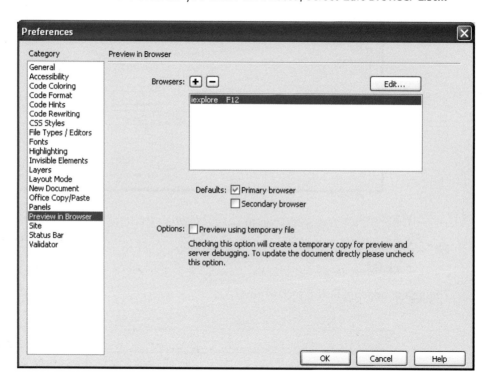

Figure 3.18: Changing browser settings using the preferences window

Tip: Other browsers include **Netscape** and **Opera**.

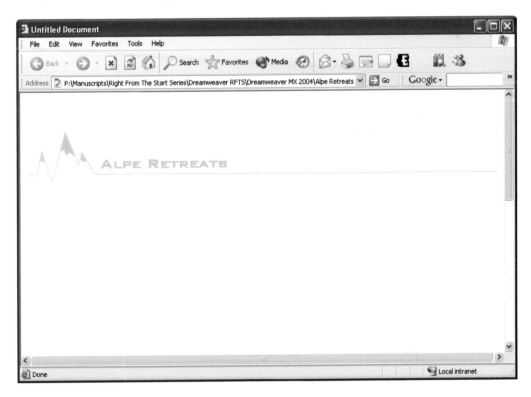

The Preferences window appears. To add a browser, just click the small + button at the top of the window. You'll then be asked to locate the browser software on your computer. You can also select a shortcut key for the new browser (F12 is the default shortcut for Internet Explorer). Click OK when you're done.

Figure 3.19: Previewing the template in Internet Explorer

This is exactly how you would view any page you create in Dreamweaver.

You can leave the browser window open while you work on the page in Dreamweaver, but it won't update to reflect any changes you make in Dreamweaver. Each time you make a change, you will need to run through the steps above to preview the page.

Borders

Notice that the borders of the cells in the table are invisible. We'll just quickly run through the different options you could choose. You may not like the look of visible borders, but they can sometimes be useful.

○   Return to the Dreamweaver window. Select the table using the <table> tag, and look at the table properties.

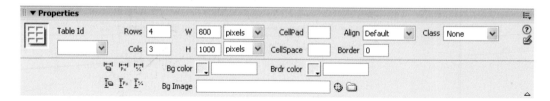

Figure 3.20: Table properties

The properties that affect the table borders are:

CellPad

Cell padding is the space around the contents of a cell.

CellSpace

Cell spacing is the space between cells in the table.

Border

You can enter a value for the border. Entering 0 gives an invisible border. The higher the number the thicker the border around the table. The default value is 1.

Brdr Color

You can choose a border colour for the whole table, a row or a cell. Remember if you want a coloured border you'll have to change the Border value to 1; if it is 0 you won't see it!

BgColor

You can change the background colour in the table, a row or an individual cell.

Changing the background colour

We'll change the colour of one of the cells.

▶   Click in the last cell in row 3.

▶   In the Properties inspector at the bottom of the screen, click the small grey square labelled Bg.

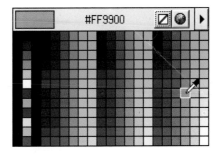

Figure 3.21: The colour palette

▶   A dropper appears. You can select any colour on your screen with this – you aren't restricted to using one in the colour palette. Choose a colour of your own, or click the orange colour as shown above.

> **Tip:** Colours chosen from the palette are **Web Safe**, meaning they will look the same on any browser. A blend of colours on the other hand, such as from the Colour Picker, is not guaranteed.

Figure 3.22

The cell is now coloured orange.

Assets and Favourites

In the Files panel group there is the Assets panel. The Assets panel contains every image, colour etc that you use in your web page. You can also make any asset a Favourite. We're going to add a colour to the Favourites.

◐ Click the Assets panel in the Files panel group. Click the Images icon on the left of the panel. At the top of the panel make sure Site is selected as shown in Figure 3.23 and not Favourites.

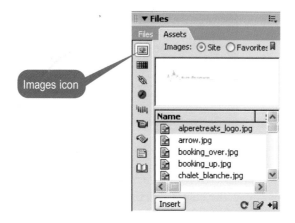

Figure 3.23: The Assets panel

Take a look at what's there. It has listed all the images in the Images folder.

◐ In the Assets panel, click the Colours icon on the left. Notice that the colour you chose may not yet have been added to the Assets panel. You need to refresh the panel first.

◐ Refresh the panel by clicking the Refresh icon at the bottom of the panel.

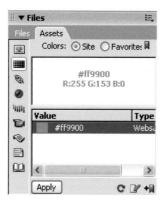

Figure 3.24: The Assets panel lists the colours used

The orange colour has now appeared in the Assets panel. Now we're going to add the grey-purple colour of the logo to the Assets panel. This grey is not in the colour palette so we'll use the dropper to click on the actual logo.

Click in the first cell in row 3. Now scroll up so that the Alpe Retreats logo is visible. Click the grey square labelled **Bg** in the **Properties** inspector.

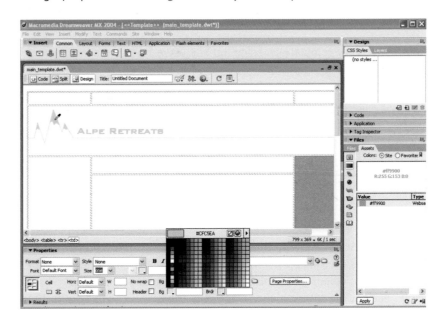

Figure 3.25: Using the dropper to select a colour outside the colour palette

Now click on the **Alpe Retreats** logo with the dropper as shown above.

Refresh the **Assets** panel. The grey-purple colour should appear alongside the orange.

Adding to Favourites

Adding any assets to **Favourites** is very straightforward. This is useful when you have so many assets that it is difficult to find any particular one. You would add an asset to **Favourites** if it was going to be used more than the others.

Click on the grey-purple colour in the **Assets** window. Click the **Add to Favourites** icon at the bottom of the panel.

Figure 3.26: Adding to Favourites

- Click OK to the above message. Click the Favourites radio button at the top of the Assets panel. The grey colour should be there.

- Add the orange colour as well. These two colours will be used as the theme for the site, and will be used again.

- Save your template by selecting File, Save from the menu. Select OK at the prompt about editable regions.

Using Favourite colours

The way you use Favourites depends on the type of asset you are applying the colour to.

- For objects, select the object, select the colour in the Favourites panel and click the Apply button.

- For background colours it works slightly differently. You can't just select the cell then the colour and click apply. Instead, make sure the Favourites panel is showing the colour you want, select a cell in the table, then click Bg in the Properties inspector. Use the dropper to click on the colour in the Favourites panel. This is most useful when you want a custom colour (that you have previously added to Favourites), and nothing else on the page is the same colour, so the only thing you can click with the dropper is in the Favourites panel.

Finish off the colour scheme to look like the one below.

Figure 3.27

- Save the template by selecting File, Save from the menu, then preview it by pressing the F12 key.

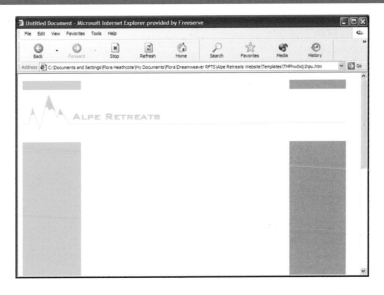

Figure 3.28

Editable Regions

When you base a web page on a template, all content that is not specifically made an editable region is locked. As a result, in order to be able to add any content to the page, you need to specify editable regions on the template.

We will define two editable regions in the centre of the template so that content can be added in the white area below the logo.

○ Click in the centre cell in row 3.

○ In the Insert bar at the top of the screen, make sure the Common tab is selected.

Note: Select the **Templates** tab if you're using version MX.

○ Click the Templates icon down-arrow.

○ Click Editable Region. You are now asked to enter a name for the editable region.

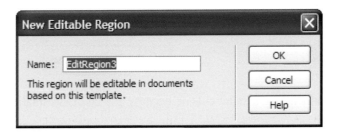

Figure 3.29: Naming an editable region

○ Enter PageTitle in the Name box. Click OK.

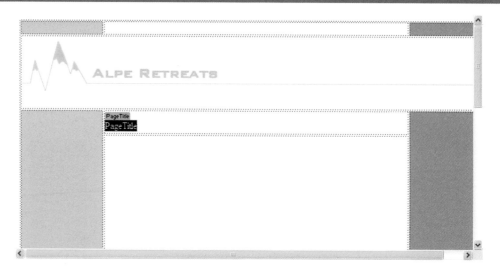

Figure 3.30

○   Repeat this for the cell below, naming the editable region PageContent.

> **Tip:** The **Templates** icon will have changed to the **Editable Region** icon because that was the last option used.

The second editable region will appear quite low down the page because it has been put in the middle of a very long cell. We'll re-align the editable regions to be at the top of each cell.

Aligning cell content

The editable regions appear in the centre of each cell because the properties of the cell specify that the contents should be aligned in the centre. It is not because of the properties of the editable regions.

○   Click somewhere in the blank area of the cell containing the first editable region (PageTitle). Now click the <td> tag in the tag selector.

○   In the Properties inspector, change the Vert property from Default to Top.

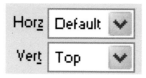

You will only notice a small change because the cell is so small.

○   Repeat this for the second editable region (PageContent). This time you should notice a big change of position, as the editable region moves to the top of the cell.

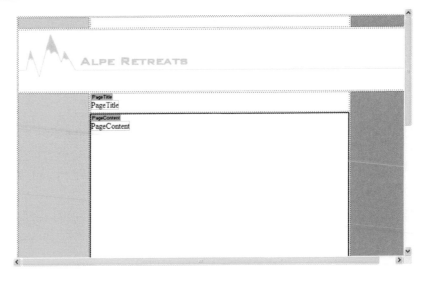

Figure 3.31

CSS Styles

CSS stands for Cascading Style Sheet. Each style sheet can contain many different styles. For this website we will use just one style sheet which will contain three text styles. It is possible to export a style sheet so that you can use the styles in other websites you design, but we won't go into that here.

> **Tip:** Although in this book we will use CSS Styles just for text, they are actually used to set the style for all sorts of things including table borders, background colours and more. There's plenty of information about them in the **Dreamweaver Help** – just look up **CSS** in the Index.

First we'll create a new style then apply it to the PageTitle text.

 Make sure you can see the CSS Styles panel in the Design panel group. If not, select Window, CSS Styles from the main menu bar.

Click the New CSS Style icon at the bottom of the CSS Styles panel.

The New CSS Style window appears.

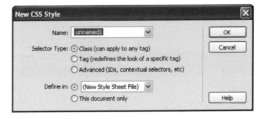

Figure 3.32: Naming a style

Note: Version MX 2004 uses CSS (Cascading Style Sheet) styles only. There are no HTML styles as in previous versions (although you can use **Tags**). CSS Styles are held in a style sheet file.

▶   Enter the style name as PageTitle and make sure that the (New StyleSheet File) option button is selected next to Define In. Click OK.

The PageTitle style we are about to create needs to be put in a style sheet. Since we don't have a style sheet created yet we need to create one.

It's a good idea to keep style sheets in a separate folder, even though we will only use one style sheet in this site.

▶   In the Save Style Sheet File As window, make a new folder called StyleSheets in the Alpe Retreats Website folder. Save this style sheet as TextStyles and set the Relative to box to Document.

Tip: Use the **New Folder** icon to create a folder.

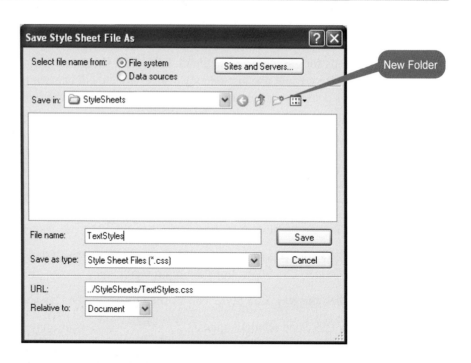

Figure 3.33: Saving a CSS file

Note: It is important to set the **Relative to** value to **Document**.

▶   Click Save.

The CSS Style Definition window appears. We can now set the properties of the PageTitle style.

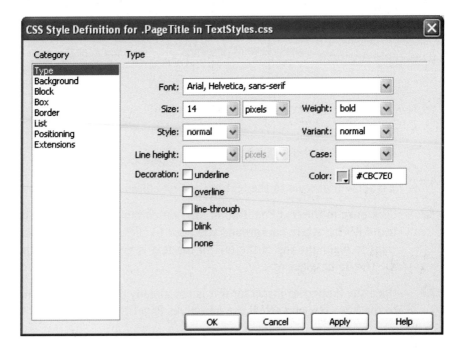

Figure 3.34: Defining a new CSS Style

Note: Notice in the **Category** list on the left of the **CSS Style Definition** window that you can set properties for all sorts of other objects, not just text.

○   Change the colour of the text by clicking the small Color box on the right. The cursor will change to a small dropper; click the dropper on the grey-purple colour we have used in the left-hand margin of the template page.

○   Set the other parameters shown above and click OK. The style now appears in the CSS Styles panel. Notice also that there is a page tab for the TextStyles.css sheet alongside the main_template.dwt tab at the top left of the page.

Tip: If you accidentally double-click the style sheet you might find that you are faced with some rather unfriendly looking code! This is because you have selected the **TextStyles.css** page; to escape this simply click the **main_template.dwt** tab at the top of the page.

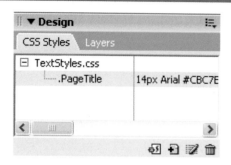

Figure 3.35: The CSS Styles panel

Now we'll apply that style to the text in the first editable region.

○   Click once in the text PageTitle in the first editable region so that it is selected (it is the text with the white background you need to click, not the green background). We don't want to highlight any of the text; if the text is highlighted black then click once more in the text to deselect it.

○   Open the Properties Inspector if it is not already open. Click the small down-arrow next to the Style box and select the new style, PageTitle from the list.

> **Tip:** If your **Properties** inspector is only displaying the Name property then you have probably selected the text (so that it is highlighted black). If so, just click once on the highlighted text to deselect it. Leave the cursor in the text field.

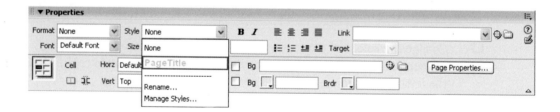

Figure 3.36

The style of the text changes, and takes on the properties of the PageTitle style.

Now we'll do the same for the PageContent text.

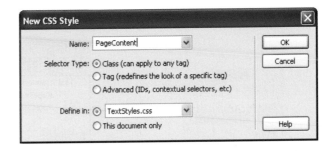 ○ Click the New CSS Style icon in the CSS Styles panel.

○ Enter the name as PageContent. We want this style to be added to the TextStyles sheet that we created, so make sure this is selected in the Define In box. Click OK.

Figure 3.37: Defining the PageContent style

○ Copy the style properties from the screenshot below:

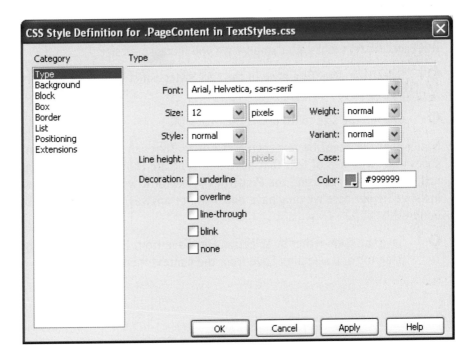

Figure 3.38

> **Tip:** You can type in the colour code next to the **Color** box instead of using the dropper. The grey we will use has the code **#999999**.

◉   Now apply the PageContent style to the text in the second editable region, just as you did the first.

The text and the CSS Styles panel should now look like those below:

Figure 3.39

Editing an existing style

The PageTitle text looks a bit small – we will increase its size.

◉   Select the .PageTitle style in the CSS Styles panel then click the Edit Style icon at the bottom of the panel.

◉   Change the size to 16 pixels then click OK.

Notice that the PageTitle text increases in size. That's the really convenient thing about preset styles – all instances of text that have that style are changed when you update the style. If you had changed the size using the Properties inspector it would have changed only that particular instance (in our case we only have one instance anyway, but in larger websites you might have hundreds!).

◉   Save the page either by selecting File, Save from the menu or by right-clicking on its page tab and selecting Save from the context menu.

Adding a Navigation bar

The best place to put a navigation bar is on the template – then it automatically appears on every page on your site (assuming every page uses the template).

We want the navigation bar to appear down the left of the page, in the grey area.

- ▶ Click in the large grey cell on the left of the template.

- ▶ On the Insert bar, click the down-arrow by the Images icon (under the Common tab).

Note: In version MX the **Navigation Bar** icon has its own spot on the **Insert** bar.

- ▶ Select Navigation Bar from the list.

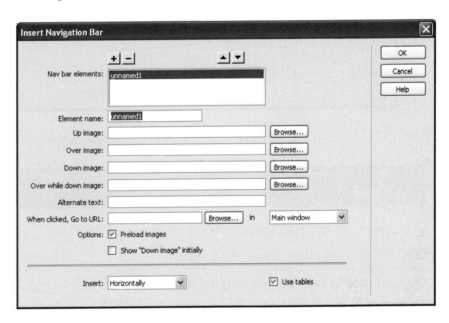

Figure 3.40: Inserting a Navigation Bar

Each nav bar Element is basically a button, or option. We're going to have 6 buttons (or elements).

For each element you need to specify a name, and which image is displayed when the button is up, down or when the mouse is over it. You will have downloaded all the necessary images in Chapter 2.

- ▶ The first button will be the Home button. Enter Home as the Element Name.

- ▶ Click the Browse button next to the Up image box.

- ▶ The image you want is in Images, nav_bar_buttons.

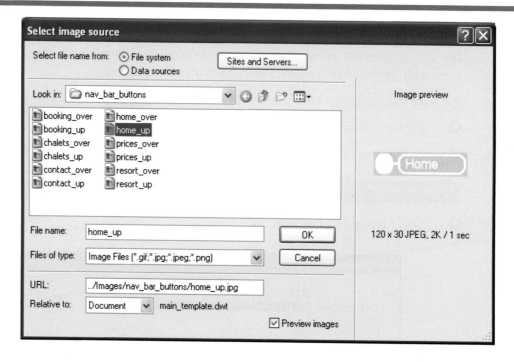

Figure 3.41: Inserting a Nav bar image

Important: Relative To should be set to **Document** not **Site Root**. The **URL** above will then start **../**

- ○ Locate the home_up image. Select it and then click OK.
- ○ For the Over Image, select home_over.

You don't need to enter any more images, Dreamweaver will automatically use the Up Image (home_up) for any of the conditions for which you haven't specified an image.

Since we haven't created the Home page yet, we won't enter a URL in the When Clicked, Go To URL field just yet – we can come back and do this later.

Adding an element

- ○ To add another button, just click the plus button at the top of the window.
- ○ Enter Resort as the name.
- ○ Enter the Up Image and Over Image as resort_up and resort_over.

Entering all the other elements

▶ Enter the other 4 elements: Chalets, Prices, Booking and Contact. Use the images with the relevant names in the nav_bar_buttons folder.

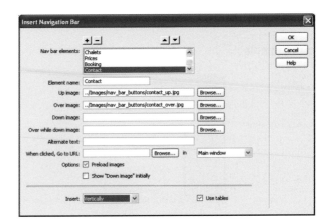

Figure 3.42: Inserting a nav bar

▶ When you have entered all the elements, change the Insert option at the bottom of the screen to Vertically. Make sure the Use Tables option is checked. Click OK.

> **Tip:** The **Insert** option at the bottom of the screen is only shown the first time you open this window. If you have already created the nav bar and are using this window to edit it you won't get this option.

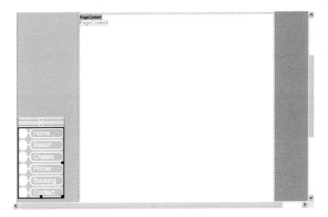

Figure 3.43

The navigation bar appears – but rather low down!

❶ If you didn't get the option to insert the nav bar vertically, or you forgot to select it: Insert a table **1** column X **6** rows where the nav bar should be. Click and drag each button from its current position into a row in the table. Resize the table cells so that the nav bar looks like the one above.

○ Shift the nav bar up to the top of the cell by changing the properties of the cell. The easiest way to do this is to click on the nav bar then click the <td> tag to select the whole cell (the cell that contains the whole nav bar – not one of the cells that makes up the nav bar). Now adjust the Vert property of the cell in the Properties inspector to Top.

○ Adjust the width of the cell to just cover the nav bar.

○ Save the template.

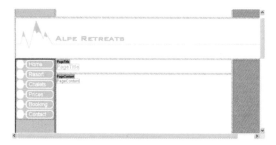

Figure 3.44

Tip: You might find that the background colour in the cell doesn't quite match the background colour of the buttons in the navigation bar. If so, select the whole cell using the **<td>** tag then change the colour using the Properties inspector – click the dropper on the grey-purple colour of the navigation bar. Do the same for the top left cell in the table.

Testing!

○ Preview your template in a browser (press F12 for Internet Explorer).

○ Move the mouse over each of the buttons – the image should change to one with an orange dot inside the white one! If it doesn't, you'll get a chance to edit your nav bar in a minute.

Note: If a button only shows a cross, Dreamweaver cannot find the image file(s). Double-click the button in Design mode and set **Relative to: Document.**

Figure 3.45

○ Close the browser window.

Editing the nav bar

If you want to change the order of the buttons, or the images, you'll need to edit your nav bar.

 ▶ Click the Nav Bar icon on the Insert bar (you shouldn't need to use the down-arrow this time, the icon has probably changed to the Nav Bar icon because it was the last icon used).

Figure 3.46

▶ Click OK to the message that appears. Make any adjustments you need to, then click OK.

 Tip: If you want to change the order of the buttons you can do this easily in the **Modify Navigation Bar** window. Just click on an element and use the small arrow icons above the **Nav Bar Elements** list to move the element up or down the list.

Saving and closing the template

▶ Select File, Save from the main menu bar.

To close the template, *either*

▶ Make sure the template page is selected then select File, Close from the menu.

or

▶ Right-click the template page tab and select Close from the shortcut menu.

You will also need to close the TextStyles.css sheet.

▶ Again, right-click the page tab for the style sheet and select Close from the menu.

Exiting Dreamweaver

▶ Close Dreamweaver by first making sure all pages are closed, then selecting File, Exit from the menu.

You'll be pleased to hear that you've finished making the template! The next step is to create some pages that are based on this template.

 Tip: You can also close Dreamweaver by clicking the red **Close** icon in the top right-hand corner of the window.

Creating the
Home Page

4

You've created the template that all the pages in your site will be based on. The first page we'll create will be the Home page.

◉   Load Dreamweaver (look back at the start of Chapter 2 if you need reminding how).

Dreamweaver may have opened a new page called Untitled-1 when it was loaded. If so we'll close it now without saving.

◉   Right-click the Untitled-1 page tab. Select Close from the context menu.

Now we'll open a new page based on the template.

◉   Select File, New from the menu.

◉   Click the Templates tab; the text will change to New From Template in the top of the window.

◉   Choose the same settings as shown below.

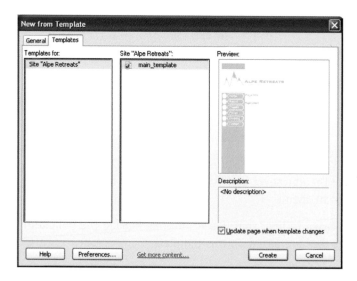

Figure 4.1: Opening a new page based on a template

◉   Click Create.

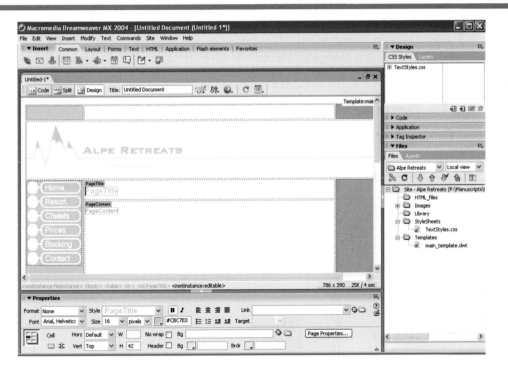

Figure 4.2

> Try changing any part of the template that you didn't specify as Editable – it will be locked.

Adding text

We're going to insert the page title in the first editable region.

> Click where it says Page Title (with the white background, not blue). Delete the text PageTitle and type Home.

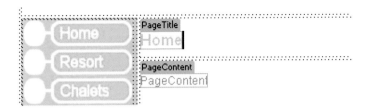

Figure 4.3

Inserting a table

Now we'll insert a table into the second editable region to help arrange the page better.

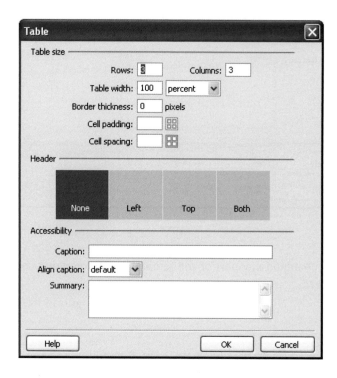

- Delete the text PageContent. Leave the cursor in the editable region.
- Click the Table icon in the Insert bar.
- Enter the settings as shown below in the top of the dialogue box. Click OK.

Figure 4.4: Inserting a table

Saving the Home page

▶ Right-click the page tab (called something like Untitled-1) and select Save from the menu.

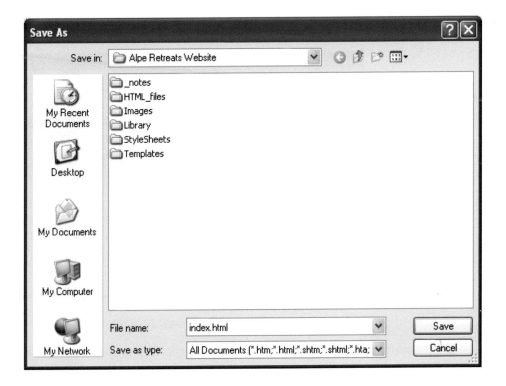

Figure 4.5

ℹ Whilst most of your html files should be saved in the HTML_files folder, many servers like the home page file to be in the root directory – that is in the Alpe Retreats Website folder.

▶ Locate the Alpe Retreats Website folder, name the file index.html and click Save. It is extremely important that you save the file with that name because nearly all servers will look for a file called index.html to display when a user logs on to the site. If you don't have a file named index.html (or index.htm) you'll just get a blank page instead of the Home page.

> **Tip:** Don't forget to include the **.html** file extension. If you leave this off Dreamweaver will add the extension **.htm**. This isn't a big problem, but it is safer to use **.html**. If you have saved the file as a **.htm** file, right-click the file in the **Files** panel and select **Rename** from the context menu.

Inserting an Image

Click the cursor in the last cell in row 2 of the new table. We need the Image icon on the Insert bar, but it may not be visible because it shares a spot with other icons. If you can't see it, click the down arrow next to the 5th icon along, and select Image from the list that appears.

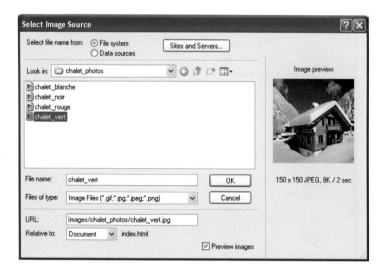

Figure 4.6: Inserting an image

Locate the chalet_vert. file under Images, chalet_photos. Select it and then click OK.

The image probably hasn't been put exactly where you want it. Adjust the table borders to look like the screenshot below.

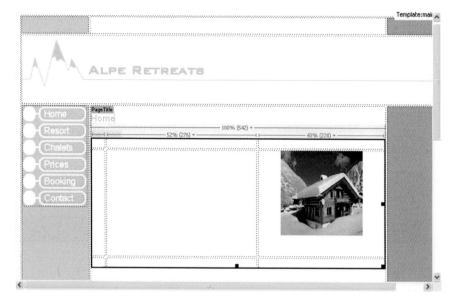

Figure 4.7: Inserting an image

ℹ You can make the image appear in the middle of the cell by placing the cursor in the cell then clicking the <td> tag in the tag selector. Change the Horiz and Vert options in the Properties inspector.

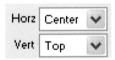

Figure 4.8

▶ Now add some text next to the picture. Either make up your own or copy the following screenshot.

ℹ To add text, just click the cursor where you want the text to appear, then start typing! If the cursor appears in the wrong place, you may have to change the Horiz and Vert settings in the Properties inspector. We'll format the text to look better later on.

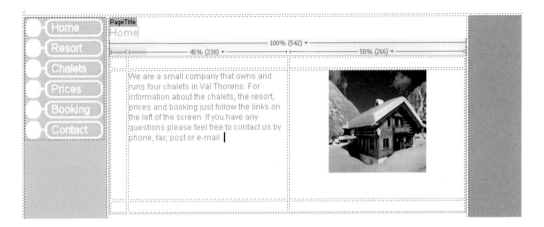

Figure 4.9: Entering text

Tip: In version MX you will find that the text is not in the correct style when you enter it. To apply the **PageContent** style, select the whole cell using the **<td>** tag then click **PageContent** in the **HTML Styles** panel.

E-mail links

Look at the last sentence in Figure 4.9; we're going to make the word e-mail a hyperlink that opens a new e-mail to a specified e-mail address.

◉   Select the text e-mail.

 ◉   Click the Email Link icon on the Insert bar.

Figure 4.10: Inserting an e-mail link

◉   Enter the information as in Figure 4.10, or alternatively enter your own e-mail address. Click OK.

The text should now be blue and underlined – this is the standard way of displaying a hyperlink.

◉   Save and preview your home page.

Figure 4.11

The orange stripe down the right of the page may be squashed. This is because the table in the second editable region has a width of 100%; when you preview the page in the browser it is trying to resize to be the width of the browser window. If we change the width to be in pixels it won't do this.

○   In Dreamweaver, select the table in the second editable region using the <table> tag.

 ○   Click the Convert Table Widths to Pixels icon in the Properties inspector.

○   Save and preview the page again. This time the orange stripe should be the same width as it is in Dreamweaver.

Test it!

○   Click the text e-mail while you're previewing your page in a browser. A new window appears where you can write and send an e-mail to the address you entered above.

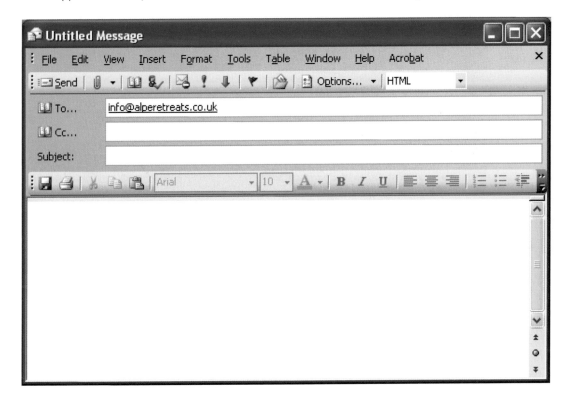

Figure 4.12: Testing the e-mail link

 ○   Try sending the e-mail if you like. Otherwise close the window by clicking the red Close icon. Keep the browser window open.

> **Tip:** An e-mail client must be set up for this to work. To do this, open **Internet Explorer** then select **Tools**, **Internet Options** from the menu. Under the **Programs** tab, make sure there is a program selected for e-mail, such as **Outlook Express**.

Adding a Page Title

Notice that in the top of the browser window it says Untitled Document. If you enter a Page Title it will appear here. This not only looks good, but is also quite important if you want your page to be picked up by search engines, as they will list search results under the Page Title of the page.

Figure 4.13: No page title

○ Return to Dreamweaver. Notice that in the Document toolbar (at the top of the page) there is a field named Title that is currently saying Untitled Document.
(If you cannot see the Document toolbar, select View, Toolbars, Document from the main menu bar).

Figure 4.14: Entering a page title in Dreamweaver

Tip: When using a Search Engine, have you ever seen entries listed under a title starting with **Untitled?**
This is because whoever created that page did not add a page title!

○ Change the Title to Alpe Retreats - Home. Now save the page and preview it again to see the effect.

Figure 4.15

Tip: If you already have a browser window open that is showing your home page try clicking the **Refresh** icon in your browser window instead of pressing **F12** again.

Design and Code View

If you really want to see the HTML code that is behind your web page you must be in the correct view.

On the Document toolbar at the top of the screen there are three different View icons:

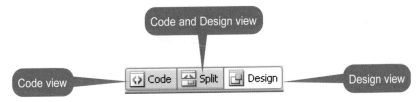

Figure 4.16: Different views

So far you have been working in Design view. This gives you the most accurate picture of how your web page will look in a Browser.

Code view shows you just the HTML code. This code will have been created by Dreamweaver, but you can edit the code directly here if you know what you're doing!

Split view splits the window in two. In the top half is the Code view and in the bottom half the Design view. You can change the size of the two windows by clicking and dragging the border between the top and bottom window.

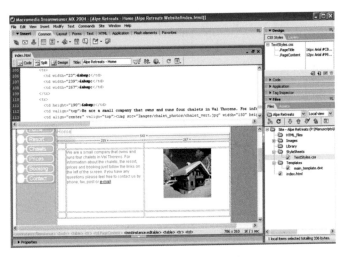

Figure 4.17: Code and Design View

Save and close the Home page

○ Save the Home page by right-clicking the page tab and selecting Save from the context menu. If the option to Save is greyed-out, this is because the page is already saved.

○ Close the page by selecting Close from the same context menu. Close any browser windows that are open.

○ Close Dreamweaver if this is the end of a session.

Creating the
Resort Page

○ First make sure that Dreamweaver is open.

○ Select File, New from the menu.

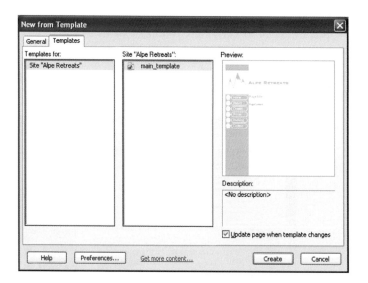

Figure 5.1: Opening a new page based on a template

○ Set the options as they are in the screenshot above then click Create.

○ Replace the text PageTitle with the text Resort.

Now you need to build the bulk of the page. The main steps you need to go through are listed below; if you can't remember how to do something, just look back over the last few chapters – you've already covered everything you need.

○ Create the table (5 rows x 3 columns) in the second editable region, and edit it so that it is the right shape by dragging the table borders. It will look better if the table is invisible so enter a Border value of 0. Remember that if you leave the width as 100% the table can obscure the orange stripe on the right of the page; convert the table widths to pixels. Don't worry about the heights of the cells, these will resize to fit the text you will type in.

○ Then enter the text – you can either copy the screenshot or just make up your own. Make sure all the text is in the right style. Don't forget to delete the text that says PageContent.

○ Save the page as Resort.html in the HTML_files folder by selecting File, Save from the menu.

○ Now insert the images to go with each paragraph of text. The file names of the images you need are labelled in the screenshot below, and are in the Images folder.

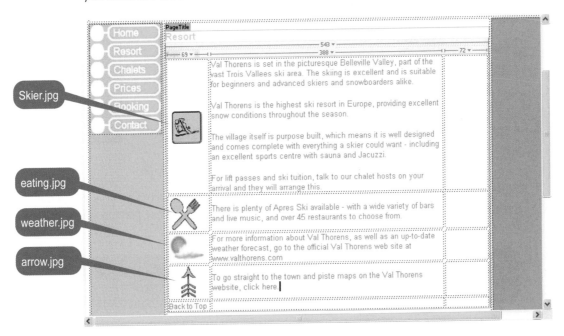

Figure 5.2

Tip: You can resize images by first selecting them so that small black handles appear. Hold down the **Shift** key then click and drag one of the corner handles. Release the mouse when you're happy with the size. If you're resizing the table borders.

○ We want the text to be spread out vertically so that not all of it fits on the screen at any one time. Select the whole table using the <table> tag then click and drag the bottom handle to make it about as long as the template.

○ Save the page again.

○ Preview your site in a browser to see how it looks.

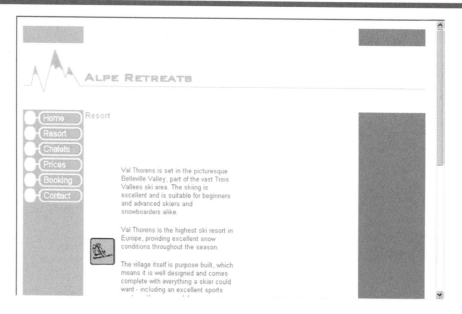

Figure 5.3: Previewing the Resort page

Looking good! Don't worry that there is a lot of wasted space on the page – this is deliberate because we need the text to be long in order to show exactly what **Named Anchors** are useful for. We'll do this now.

Tip: If you find that when trying to resize cells in the table that the borders refuse to budge in a particular direction, try first moving them in the opposite direction first, then back to where you want them. I don't know why this works but it does!

Named Anchors

There is quite a lot of text on this page, and if previewed in a small browser window people would have to scroll down to the information they are interested in. **Named Anchors** allow you to click on a menu item at the top of a page and be taken to a specific place on the same page.

- In Dreamweaver, place the cursor at the end of the text in the top editable region (where it says **Resort**) and press **Enter** to get a new line.

- Enter the text as shown below (**Resort | Apres Ski | Weather | Maps**). Highlight the text you have just typed in (don't select the **Resort** title). In the **Properties** inspector select the **PageContent** style using the **Style** option.

Figure 5.4

Now we'll insert the anchors.

- Place the cursor to the left of the first word in the first paragraph (i.e. to the left of Val Thorens)

- Click the Named Anchor icon on the Insert bar.

Figure 5.5: Creating a Named Anchor

- Enter Resort and click OK.

A small anchor symbol will appear where the cursor was. This won't appear in a browser – it will be invisible.

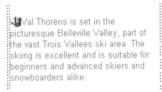

Figure 5.6: The anchor is shown in Dreamweaver but will be invisible in a browser

- Repeat this for the 3 other paragraphs, naming the anchors ApresSki, Weather and Maps.

Now we need to set up hyperlinks to link the words at the top with each anchor.

- Double-click on the word Resort (the one with the PageContent style, not the PageTitle style) in the first editable region. Look at the Properties inspector at the bottom of the screen; there is a property called Link that should currently be blank.

Figure 5.7: The Link property is used to create hyperlinks

○ Click and drag the target symbol next to the Link field onto the first named anchor symbol, so that it says #Resort in the Link field, then drop.

> **Tip:** You could also have just typed in **#Resort** instead of using the drag and drop method.

○ Repeat this for the other 3 items, ApresSki, Weather and Maps.

○ Finally, create a named anchor at the top of the screen and then link the Back to Top text (at the bottom of the page) to it.

○ Test it! Save the page and preview it in a browser. Click on all the links you've just created.

Hyperlinks to other websites

Notice that in the Weather section there is a reference to the Val Thorens official website. We are going to make a hyperlink that will open the Val Thorens website in a new browser window.

○ Select the text www.valthorens.com. We need to enter the website address in the Link field in the Properties inspector.

○ Type in the text http://www.valthorens.com in the Link field in the Properties inspector.

Figure 5.8: The Link property

> **Tip:** You cannot just enter **www.valthorens.com**, you have to enter the **http://** bit too, because it is an external site.

Opening the site in another window

At the moment the hyperlink is opening the new site in the same window – effectively closing your site!

○ Select the Val Thorens hyperlink on the page. In the Properties inspector select _blank from the menu in the Target field. Selecting _blank always means that the link will open in a new (blank) window.

Figure 5.9: Opening a link in a new window

Save the page then preview it to see that the links work properly. You'll need to be online to check the external links.

Figure 5.10: The Val Thorens website in October

The Maps link

Notice that it says in the maps info to click here to go straight to the maps part of the Val Thorens site. This link should actually link to a specific page within the Val Thorens website. You can do this by logging on to the Val Thorens website (www.valthorens.com), going to the Maps page then copying the address in the Address bar. You can then paste this address into the Link field in the Properties inspector.

The website address is http://www.valthorens.com/hiver/uk/plans.asp?plan=station – quite a mouthful! This is why it's often easier to use copy and paste rather than trying to type it.

Test the link. Save and close the Resort page.

Accessibility

There are things you can add to your website to make it much easier to use for someone who is blind or partially-sighted. There is software available that will read text on a screen, and any other text you might have hidden on the page for this purpose. For example, you can attach text to an image that can be read out to someone browsing your site. In fact, you can attach text to a variety of objects in Dreamweaver.

○ Select Edit, Preferences from the menu bar.

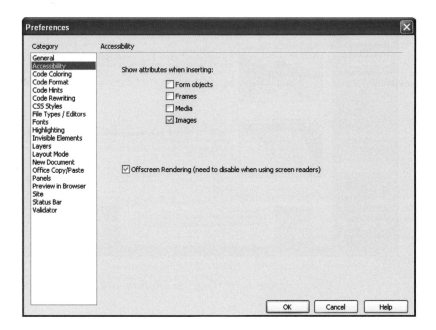

Figure 5.11: Accessibility options in the Preferences window

○ Check the boxes next to the objects that you want to add alternative text to. Just select Images to begin with. Click OK.

○ Open up the index.html page. Delete the chalet photo chalet_vert.jpg and re-insert it.

Figure 5.12: Adding accessibility features to an image

○ The Image Tag Accessibility Attributes window appears. Type something suitable in the Alternative Text and Long Description fields. Click OK.

○ Save the page.

How accessible is your site?

Dreamweaver can generate a report listing all the parts of the page that aren't deemed accessible.

◉ Click away from the photo you've just inserted. Select File, Check Page, Check Accessibility from the menu.

The Results panel group appears containing an accessibility report.

◉ Click and drag the border between the Properties panel and the blank workspace to make the Results panel group bigger.

> **Tip:** The red cross means that the item is not accessible. The question mark means that the item might cause some confusion.

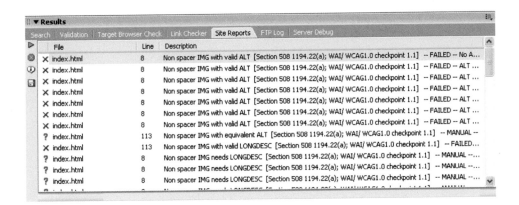

Figure 5.13: An Accessibility report

◉ There are quite a few items here! This is because none of the images in the template have alternative text. Try adding some more alternative text to the images on the template and running the report again.

> **Tip:** Close the **Results** panel group by clicking the icon at the top right of the group and selecting **Close Panel Group** from the menu

◉ Save and close any pages you have open.

Layers

6

In this chapter you'll be creating the Chalets page. Like the other pages, the bulk of the Chalets page is made up of images and text set in a table which you are already familiar with. The difference with this page is that it is actually four pages, not one (one page for each chalet). We will create a second menu that appears when the Chalets nav bar button is pressed, from which you can select the chalet you wish to see.

This will give you a useful introduction to both Layers and Behaviours, both of which might sound a bit advanced, but are really quite straightforward. The extra menu will add a professional touch to your site. Behaviours will be covered in the next chapter.

Layers

Layers are useful for two main reasons:

- They are good for layout because they allow you to overlap items and place one thing on top of another (which is not possible without layers). If an object is placed in its own layer, you can place it anywhere on the page, without using a table.

- You can attach Behaviours to layers. The Behaviours we will be using are Show and Hide. The menu layer will be hidden most of the time, and shown only when the mouse is over the Chalets nav bar button.

Creating a new layer

The new layer will be part of the template because we want it to appear alongside the nav bar on every page.

- Open the main_template.dwt file by double-clicking it in the Files panel (you may need to expand the Templates folder).

The layers are listed in the Layers panel which is in the Design panel group (Advanced Layout in version MX). As you can see there are no layers currently created.

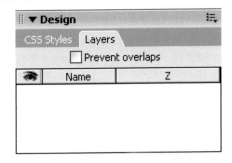

Figure 6.1: The Layers panel in the Design panel group

Tip: If you can't see the **Layers** panel, select **Window**, **Layers** from the menu. (**Window, Others, Layers** in version MX.)

● Click the Layout tab in the Insert bar.

● Insert a new layer by clicking the Draw Layer icon in the Insert bar.

Figure 6.2: The Layout tab on the Insert bar

Draw Layer

● Drag out a small rectangle as shown below.

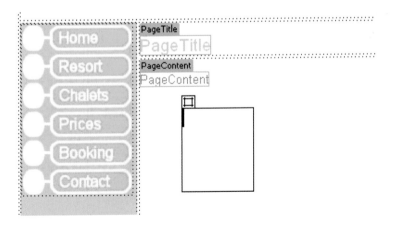

Figure 6.3: Drawing a layer

Now we'll insert a table into the new layer.

Use the Table icon on the Insert bar (there is a Table icon under the Layout tab as well as the Common tab) to insert a table 4 rows x 1 column. The cursor must be in the new layer in order that the table is inserted in the layer.

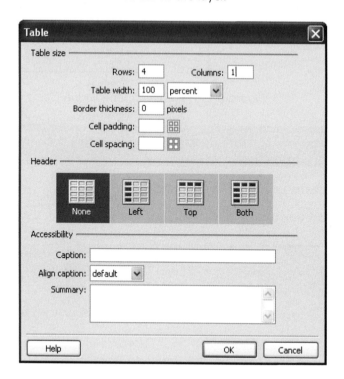

Figure 6.4: Inserting a table into a layer

Type the following text into the table:

Figure 6.5

Resizing the layer

The text in your layer might run onto 2 lines, in which case you need to widen it.

▶ If the handles are not visible, move the cursor over the edge of the layer so that it becomes a cross-headed arrow, as shown below, and click.

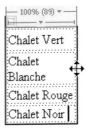

Figure 6.6: Selecting a layer

▶ You should now see small black handles around the layer. You can click and drag these handles to resize the layer.

Figure 6.7: Resizing a layer

Changing the table background colour

▶ We want to colour the background orange, but leave a white space between the cells. To do this, leave the table background settings as they are, and change the cell backgrounds individually. Just click in a cell, and change the **Bg** property in the **Properties** inspector to orange (click the dropper on a button in the nav bar to perfectly match the colours).

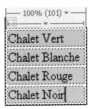

Figure 6.8: Changing the cell background colours

- Click the New CSS Style icon at the bottom right of the CSS Styles panel.

- Create a new style called LayerMenu. Select TextStyles.css from the Define In drop-down list. Click OK.

Figure 6.9

- Set the font to Arial, Helvetica, sans-serif and the size to 10 points. Change the colour to white.

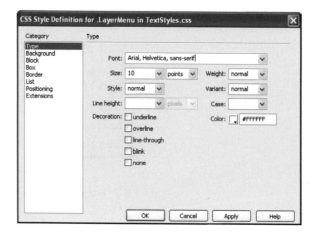

Figure 6.10

- Apply the style to each table cell.

Tip: To apply the style, check in a cell, right-click on the style and choose **Apply**.

A new page for TextStyles.css has automatically appeared next to the main_template.dwt page tab at the top of the page. We will close this page now.

- At the top of the page, right-click the page tab for the TextStyles.css file and select Close from the menu that appears. If prompted to save click Yes.

Naming the layer

It is always a good idea to name layers so that you can easily recognise which layer is which when they are listed in the **Layers** panel.

 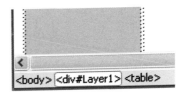

Figure 6.11: Selecting the cell to display layer properties

⊙ Select the layer either by clicking on the top left layer handle (shown above) or by using the <div#Layer1> tag to display the layer properties in the **Properties** inspector.

Figure 6.12: Layer properties

⊙ Enter **SubMenu** as the **LayerID**.

❶ If you look in the **Layers** panel the layer should now be listed under its new name.

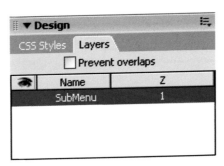

Figure 6.13: The SubMenu layer is displayed in the Layers panel

Tip: The **Layers** panel is called the **Advanced Layout** panel in version MX.

Hiding the layer

You can show and hide a layer whilst designing a site using the Layers panel.

○ In the column that has an eye in the header, click next to the layer. A closed-eye symbol will appear and the layer will disappear.

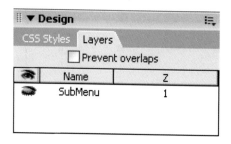

Figure 6.14: Showing and hiding a layer

○ Keep clicking in the same place; the layer will cycle through three phases: hidden, visible and unspecified. Leave the layer hidden, with the closed-eye icon.

Save!

○ Don't forget to save your work regularly. When you save you will get the following message because you have two pages based on the template. Just click Yes (Update in version MX) and then Close when the pages are updated.

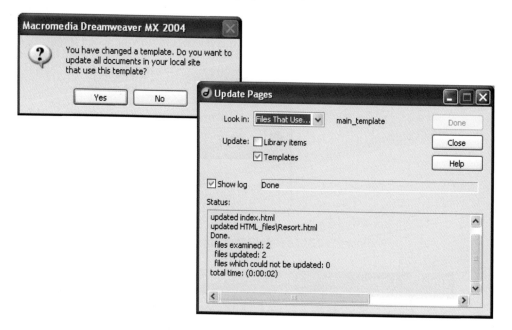

Figure 6.15: Saving a template

Creating the chalet pages

You need to create 4 new pages, each of which will be named after a chalet and will contain an image and some text about that chalet. We will then set up hyperlinks to link the menu items with each of the pages. You may need to refer to Chapter 4, where you created the Home page, as the procedure will be almost identical.

> **Tip:** When you insert the chalet photos you will probably get a prompt about **Alternative Text** – this is because you have the Image accessibility checked in **Preferences** (see page 57 to uncheck this option).

 ◗ Open 4 new pages based on the main_template, saving them as ChaletVert, ChaletBlanche, ChaletRouge and ChaletNoir. Say Yes to update links when asked.

 ◗ In the Images folder there are images for each of the chalets, named after the chalets. Insert the images and some text so that the pages look something like the one below. You will need a table.

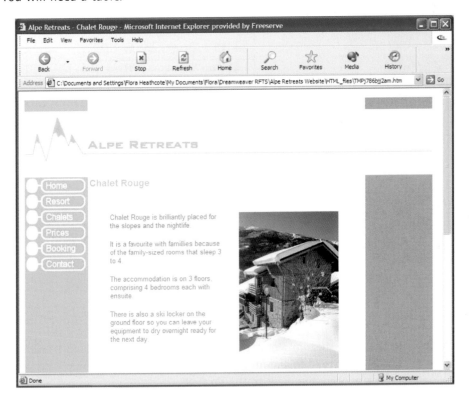

Figure 6.16: The Chalet Rouge page

> **Tip:** To speed things up, you could copy the table, text and image from the first chalet page you create and paste it into the others, changing only some of the text and the image. To do this, select the table using the **<table>** tag just above the properties panel and select **Edit**, **Copy** from the menu. Go to the second chalet page, place the cursor in the editable region and select **Edit**, **Paste** from the menu.

Save all

When you are creating and editing a lot of pages at once you can save all instead of individually saving pages.

- Select File, Save All from the menu.
- Close the four chalet pages you have just created.

Creating the hyperlinks

- Open the template (main_template.dwt) and unhide the SubMenu layer.
- Highlight the text Chalet Vert in the SubMenu layer.
- Make sure all the html files of the chalet pages are visible in the Files panel.

Figure 6.17: The Files panel

- In the Properties inspector, click and drag the target next to the Link field onto the ChaletVert.html file and drop. Be careful to select the target next to the Link field – there's another one next to the Bg field.

Tip: If you don't like using the target, click the **Browse** icon to the right of the target. Now find and select the file you want and then click **OK**.

The text should now be underlined to signify a hyperlink.

○ The text may have turned blue also – to change it back to white, just highlight it then reselect LayerMenu from the Style list in the Properties inspector.

○ Repeat this for the other menu items, linking them to the relevant chalet pages.

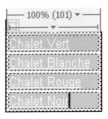

Figure 6.18: Creating hyperlinks

○ Save your template choosing Update at the prompt, then Close to close the Update Pages window. Close the template if this is the end of a session, otherwise leave it open for the next chapter.

Behaviours 7

In this chapter we'll add the behaviours that will make the SubMenu layer appear when the mouse is on the Chalets nav bar button. The submenu will disappear again when either a submenu option is selected or the mouse is no longer over the Chalets button or the SubMenu layer.

▶ Open the template if it is not already open.

▶ Click the Chalets button on the nav bar. Open the Tag Inspector panel group then click the Behaviours panel tab. See that there are already some Behaviours here that Dreamweaver created for you when you designed the nav bar.

Figure 7.1: The Behaviours panel

> **Tip:** If you can't see the **Behaviours** panel, select **Window**, **Tag Inspector** from the main menu bar.
> In version MX it is in the **Design** panel group.

Choosing a browser version

Some behaviours don't work in earlier browsers, so you can select which behaviours are available to you according to which browsers you want them to work in.

➕▾ ▶ Click the plus symbol near the top of the Behaviours panel.

> **Note**: If, when you click the plus symbol, you get a message about **Call Javascript**, just click **Cancel** then click the **plus** symbol again. I found that because this was the first item on the menu I kept selecting it accidentally!

○ Select Show Events For from the menu. You can now choose a browser. If you have it, select IE 4.0.

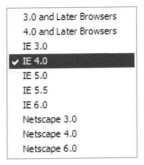

Figure 7.2: Choosing a browser version

Adding a new behaviour

○ To add a new behaviour, just click the **plus** button at the top of the **Behaviours** window.

Figure 7.3: Selecting the type of behaviour

○ Select **Show-Hide** Layers from the menu.

Figure 7.4: The Show-Hide Layers behaviour

○ Click the **Show** button at the bottom of the **Show-Hide Layers** window; (show) should appear beside the layer name. Click **OK**.

At the moment, the **Show-Hide Layers** action is dependent on the **onClick** event (this is the default option). We need to change it to **onMouseOver**.

◉ In the **Behaviours** panel, click the text **OnClick** (the last entry in the left column), then on the small down-arrow. Now select **onMouseOver** from the menu that appears.

Figure 7.5: Selecting an event to trigger the behaviour

Tip: If you go wrong, select Edit, Undo from the main menu bar.

The **Behaviours** panel should now look like this:

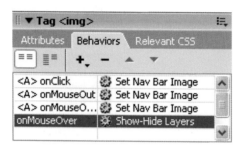

Figure 7.6: The Behaviours panel

◉ Now create another behaviour. The **Action** will be to **Hide** the **SubMenu** layer, and the **Event** will be **onMouseOut**. The method is the same as that used above, so refer to that if you get stuck. Make sure the **Chalets** nav bar button is still selected or you'll attach the behaviour to something else!

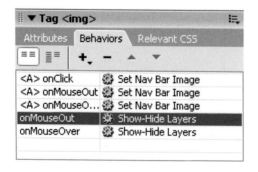

Figure 7.7: The Behaviours panel

- ► Hide the SubMenu layer using the Layers panel (so that there is a closed eye next to the layer name). Save the template.

Reminder: Advanced Layout panel in version MX.

- ► Now preview the template in a browser. The submenu should appear and disappear as you move the mouse over the Chalets button. Don't worry about the position of the layer, we'll change that later.

Adding behaviours to the layer

We will attach another couple of behaviours to the layer itself. We want to show the layer when the mouse is over the layer, and hide it if the mouse leaves the layer. What we then need to do is move the layer close enough to the Chalets button so that the mouse can be over the layer before leaving the Chalets button. If we don't do this, the layer will disappear before the mouse gets to it!

- ► Show the layer using the Layers panel so that you can work on it.

- ► Select the layer – make sure you've selected the whole layer, if so Layer ID should be displayed in the Properties inspector. The easiest way of selecting the whole layer is to select it in the Layers panel.

- ► Click the plus button in the Behaviours panel to add a new behaviour.

- ► Select Show-Hide Layers from the menu then click the Show button in the Show–Hide Layers window. Click OK.

- ► Change the Event from onClick to onMouseOver.

- ► Create a second behaviour to Hide the layer onMouseOut.

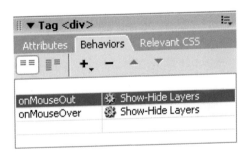

Figure 7.8: The Behaviours panel

Moving the layer

You need to move the layer so that it is just touching the **Chalets** button. This will take some trial and error, as the layer often appears in a slightly different place to where you think when you preview it in a browser!

▶ Click and drag the layer so that it is touching the **Chalets** button. Preview the page in a browser.

Tip: You can use the arrow keys on the keyboard to finely adjust the position of the layer.

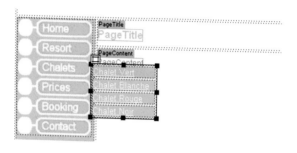

Figure 7.9: The SubMenu layer in Design view

Figure 7.10: The SubMenu layer in Preview mode

The two screenshots above show the layer in what's supposed to be the same position, in **Design** and in **Preview** mode.

▶ You also need to test that the menu doesn't disappear before the mouse reaches it (in which case you need to move the layer closer to the **Chalets** button) and that the hyperlinks work.

▶ When you are happy with the position of the layer, set it to **hidden** in the **Layers** panel so that when you preview the page it will be hidden until the mouse moves over the **Chalets** button.

▶ Save your template.

Setting up the hyperlinks for the nav bar

Since you are already editing the template, now would be a good time to enter the hyperlinks on the nav bar, for the Home and Resort pages.

○ Click the Nav Bar icon on the Insert bar to edit the existing nav bar. It might be hidden behind the Image icon – it's the 5th icon along under the Common tab. Click Yes when asked if you want to modify the existing nav bar.

○ In the Modify Navigation Bar window, click the Browse button next to the When Clicked, Go To URL: field.

○ Find the index.html file and click OK.

○ Repeat this for the Resort button, entering the appropriate URL as shown in Figure 7.11.

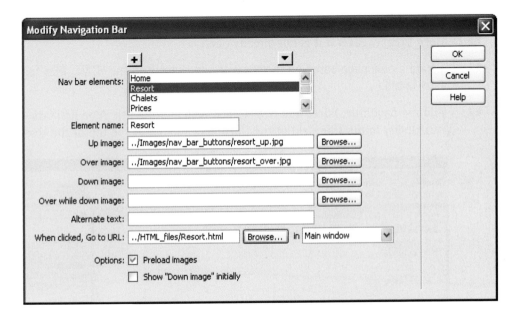

Figure 7.11: Adding hyperlinks to the nav bar

○ Repeat for the Chalets button.

○ Click OK.

Saving the template

○ Save the template and then preview it. Test that the buttons take you to the correct pages.

○ Close the template, and Dreamweaver too if this is the end of a session.

Tables of Data

8

In this chapter you'll be creating the Prices page. This is essentially a large table of data, and you have already learned most of the features you need to do this.

- Open Dreamweaver if it is not already open.

- Create a new page based on the template and save it in the HTML_files folder as Prices.html.

- Add the page title, Prices and Availability. Also add the title Alpe Retreats – Prices and Availability in the Title field of the Document toolbar at the top of the screen.

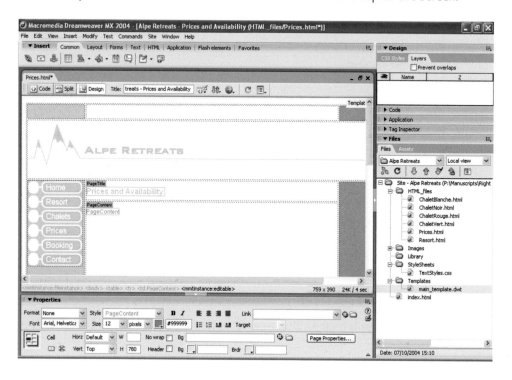

Figure 8.1: Adding the page title on the page and the toolbar

Because the prices table is quite big, quite a large table is needed. We'll create the prices table inside another table to make its positioning easier.

○ First delete the text PageContent in the second editable region.

 ○ Create the first table, 3 columns x 3 rows. Resize it so that it covers most of the page, with the centre cell much larger than the rest (see Figure 8.2). Don't forget to convert the width to pixels.

Figure 8.2

The prices table will go in the centre cell of the first table; the first table is there to help you position the prices table exactly where you want it on the page.

 ○ Place the cursor in the centre cell, then click the Insert Table icon to insert the second table.

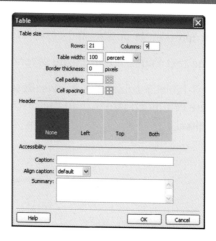

Figure 8.3: Inserting a table

○ Specify a table with **21** rows and **9** columns as shown above. Click **OK**.

○ Merge some of the cells in the top row of this table using the **Merge Cells** icon in the **Properties** inspector, so that your table looks like Figure 8.4.

> **Tip:** To merge cells, click and drag from one cell to another so as to select both cells. When both cells are highlighted click the **Merge Cells** icon. Another way of selecting two cells is to click one, then hold down the **Shift** key while you click in another cell (this might take two clicks).

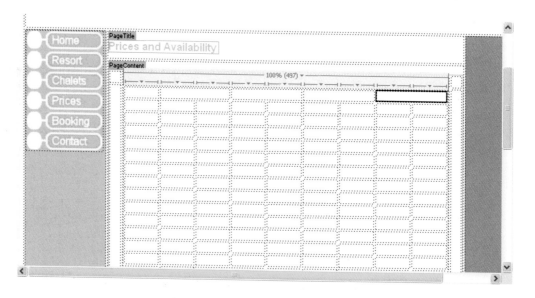

Figure 8.4: Merging cells

○ Enter the column headings, row headings and data as shown in the Figure 8.5 (it doesn't matter if you make up your own, or even if you leave some cells empty).

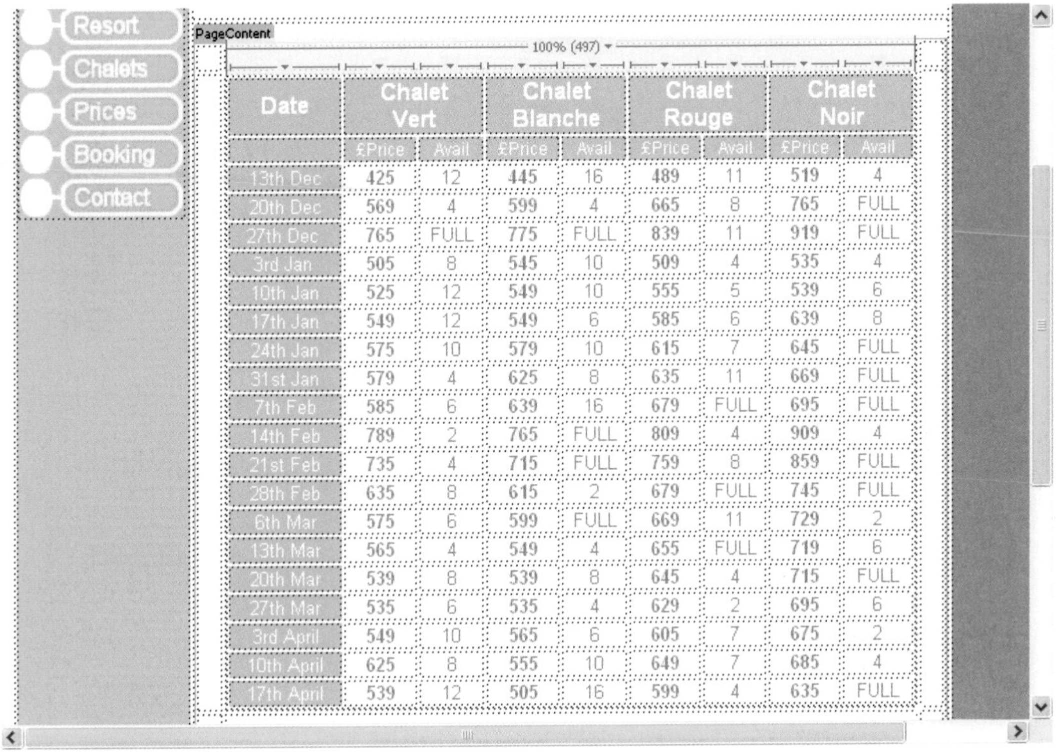

Date	Chalet Vert		Chalet Blanche		Chalet Rouge		Chalet Noir	
	£Price	Avail	£Price	Avail	£Price	Avail	£Price	Avail
13th Dec	425	12	445	16	489	11	519	4
20th Dec	569	4	599	4	665	8	765	FULL
27th Dec	765	FULL	775	FULL	839	11	919	FULL
3rd Jan	505	8	545	10	509	4	535	4
10th Jan	525	12	549	10	555	5	539	6
17th Jan	549	12	549	6	585	6	639	8
24th Jan	575	10	579	10	615	7	645	FULL
31st Jan	579	4	625	8	635	11	669	FULL
7th Feb	585	6	639	16	679	FULL	695	FULL
14th Feb	789	2	765	FULL	809	4	909	4
21st Feb	735	4	715	FULL	759	8	859	FULL
28th Feb	635	8	615	2	679	FULL	745	FULL
6th Mar	575	6	599	FULL	669	11	729	2
13th Mar	565	4	549	4	655	FULL	719	6
20th Mar	539	8	539	8	645	4	715	FULL
27th Mar	535	6	535	4	629	2	695	6
3rd April	549	10	565	6	605	7	675	2
10th April	625	8	555	10	649	7	685	4
17th April	539	12	505	16	599	4	635	FULL

Figure 8.5: Entering text and data

Tip: To make the chalet names appear on two lines hold down the **Shift** key then press **Enter**. If you don't hold down **Shift** you get a very large gap between the lines.

ⓘ Notice that the current availability is shown on this page. The availability figure will need to be updated regularly by someone at Alpe Retreats. You will learn how to update a web page later when you learn how to get your web page online.

Resizing table columns

You may need to resize the columns to fit the data on one line – the table will become twice as long if each line of data runs onto two lines.

○ Click and drag the table borders to resize the columns. This can be rather frustrating; a little time and patience should do the trick though.

◉   Finally add some text below the table as shown below.

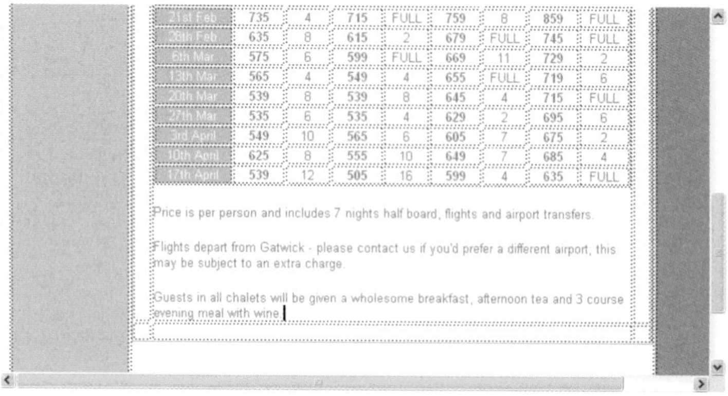

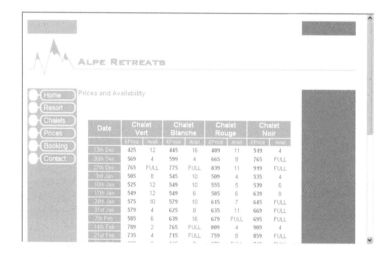

Figure 8.6

◉   Save the page then preview it in a browser to see what it looks like.

Figure 8.7: Previewing the page

Tip: If the orange border on the right is narrower when you preview the page, this is because you haven't converted the table widths to pixels. Do this then check again that the border looks OK.

That's the Prices page finished!

◉   Save and close the page.

◉   Open the main_template.dwt file and add the hyperlink for the Prices button on the nav bar. Save and preview the site and flick between all the pages you've done so far to check they work as expected.

Forms

9

In this chapter you'll create the Booking page. This will involve using Forms, which we haven't covered yet. The form will be filled in by the customer online, and then sent to the host of the Alpe Retreats site by e-mail.

The information from a form is collected in something called a script. The script can be written in a variety of programming languages, and can be sent to a specified location (including an e-mail address). There are many options here, and there may be specific reasons why you may want to use one programming language over another – one of which is the facilities provided by your ISP (Internet Service Provider). Here it will be assumed that you have an ISP that supports a script being sent to a specified e-mail address. Don't worry if you don't have an ISP – we'll cover that in the next chapter.

The form container

All the fields in a form need to be held in a form container. This is just a simple box that will expand as you put more in it.

▶   Create a new page based on the template. Save the page as Booking.html.

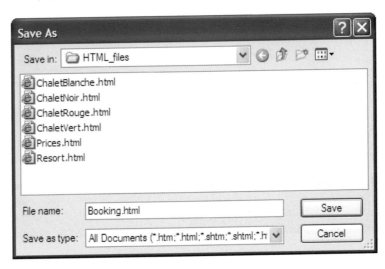

Figure 9.1: Saving a page

○ Change the Page Title to Booking in the first editable region.

> **Tip**: Don't forget to give the page a title in the **Document** toolbar at the top of the page.
> I've named mine **Alpe Retreats – Booking**.

○ Delete the text PageContent in the second editable region.

○ On the Insert bar, click the Forms tab.

Figure 9.2: The Forms section of the Insert bar

○ Click the cursor in the PageContent editable region. Press Enter to expand the editable region.

○ Click the Form icon in the Insert bar.

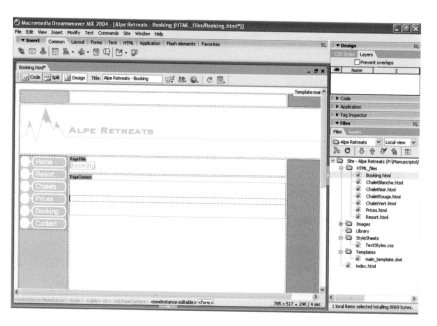

Figure 9.3: The form container is shown by a red dotted line

A red dotted line appears representing the form container. The cursor should now be inside the new form container, and the form properties should be displayed in the Properties inspector.

> **Tip:** If you can't see the red dotted line you might have **Invisible Elements** switched off.
> To turn them on, select **View**, **Visual Aids**, **Invisible Elements** from the menu bar. It will
> have a small tick next to it if it's already selected.

The best way to arrange the various elements of a form is usually to put them into a table. We'll create the table first then insert the elements in it.

Create the table

> Make sure the cursor is within the form container (<Form> will be highlighted in the Tag selector at the bottom of the page, and the form properties will be displayed in the Properties inspector). Create a table with 15 rows and 7 columns.

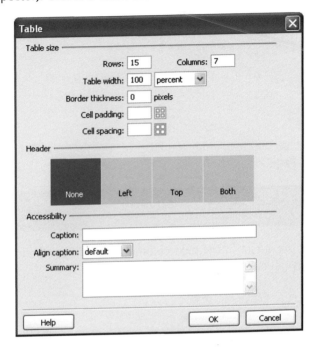

Figure 9.4: Inserting a table

Tip: The **Table** icon is on the **Layout** tab.

> Arrange the columns to look like the screenshot below.

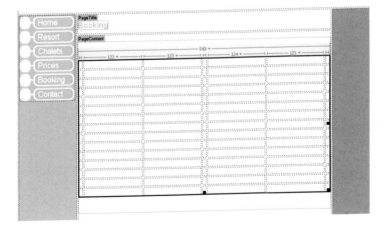

Figure 9.5

○ Merge the cells in the top row and add the following text:

Figure 9.6

Adding a text field

○ In the second row, enter the label for the first text field, **First Name**. It should have the style **PageContent**.

> **Tip:** Highlight the whole table and give it the style **PageContent**. That way, anything you type in any cell will have that style.

○ Click the cursor in the next column (column 3) and click the **Text Field** icon under the **Forms** tab on the **Insert** bar.

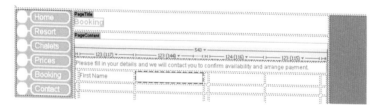

Figure 9.7: Inserting a text field

Naming fields

You should name all elements on the form. The form script will basically contain a list of field names and the values entered into these fields by the user. If you haven't named the fields this list of information will mean nothing, and will be much more difficult to process.

○ Make sure the text field you just created is selected (click it if the field properties aren't showing in the **Properties** inspector).

○ Enter **FirstName** (no spaces) into the field name box.

Figure 9.8: Naming a field

Changing the size of a text field

The text field is slightly longer than we want it. You cannot click and drag the borders of the field to resize it; instead you use the Properties inspector.

○ In the Properties inspector, set the Char Width property to 20. Press Enter.

Figure 9.9: Changing the width of a field

○ Adjust the column widths again so that the text field fills the width of the column.

Creating a List field

A List field is one where instead of typing in a value, you select it from a list. These fields are useful where there are only a limited number of values that a field can take such as a Title field.

○ In the fifth column, type Title.

  ○ Click in the next column then click the List/Menu icon on the Insert bar (make sure the Forms tab is selected).

Figure 9.10: Inserting a List field

Take a look at the List field properties:

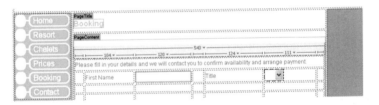

Figure 9.11: List field properties

○ Name the field Title.

These fields can be used as menus as well as lists, but for now we want it to be a simple list.

○ Click the List radio button in the Properties inspector.

Adding list values

Now you need to enter the values that will appear in the list.

- Click the List Values button in the Properties inspector.

- Enter Miss as the Item Label. Don't worry about entering a value.

- Click the + button to add another value. Type Mrs.

- Add some more options so that your list looks like the one below.

Figure 9.12: Entering item labels

> **Tip:** If you want to change the order the values appear in the list, first select a value then click the up and down arrows in the top right of the **List Values** window.

- Click OK when you are happy with the list.

- In the Properties inspector, select Mr as the Initially Selected value.

Figure 9.13: Selecting the Initially Selected value

Entering the other text and list fields

There are quite a few text fields and one list field that you now know how to create.

○ Enter the labels and create the text fields shown in the screenshot below. Make sure you give each field a meaningful name and a Char Width of 20.

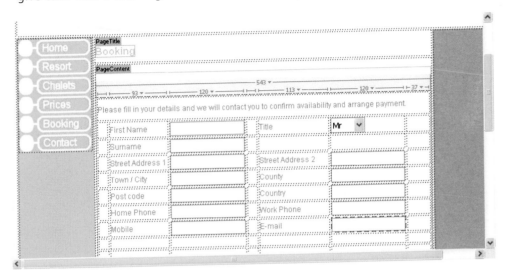

Figure 9.14

○ Create a List field for the Chalet Name field. Enter the four chalet names as the list values (Chalet Vert, Chalet Blanche, Chalet Rouge, Chalet Noir). Give the field a meaningful name. The width of the field will adjust automatically to the length of the list values you enter.

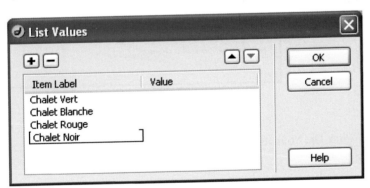

Figure 9.15: Entering List labels

○ Don't forget to save your page regularly.

Radio buttons

Radio buttons are grouped, and the user can select only one button from the group. We will use radio buttons to ask the user how they would prefer Alpe Retreats to contact them.

○ Add the labels Week Commencing and Number in Group as shown below (you can also add the text fields if you like; they have been omitted here in this sample form).

○ Enter the text from the screenshot below.

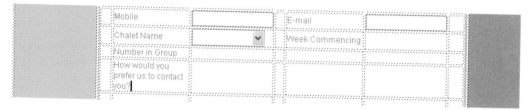

Figure 9.16

○ Click the cursor in the next column then click the Radio Group icon on the Insert bar.

○ Enter the information as it is in Figure 9.17. To enter values for the buttons, click on the word Radio in the list then type the new text. To add more buttons click the plus symbol (+).

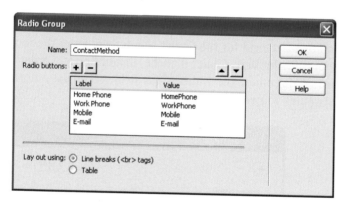

Figure 9.17: Radio Groups

○ Click OK. Your form should now look like Figure 9.18.

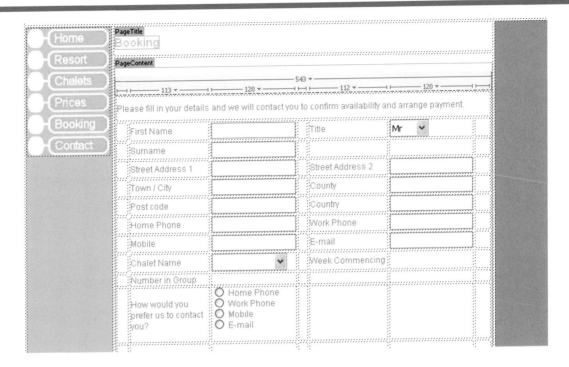

Figure 9.18: Radio Groups

▶ Save and preview your form.

Text Areas

Now we'll add a text area. This is a larger field where people can type any comments or questions they may have.

▶ Enter the text shown below, beginning **Please leave any comments...**

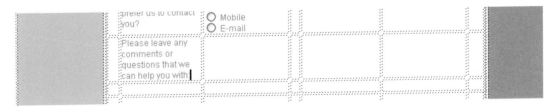

Figure 9.19

▶ Merge the next 4 columns in this row. Click in the merged cell so that the cursor is in the cell.

▶ Click the Text Area icon on the Insert bar.

▶ In the Properties inspector, adjust the Char Width to about 45 and Num Lines to 4.

Adding buttons

Finally, you need to add a couple of buttons. One of the buttons will Clear the form, and the other will Submit it.

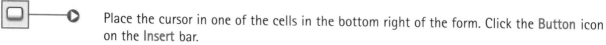

Place the cursor in one of the cells in the bottom right of the form. Click the Button icon on the Insert bar.

The button becomes a Submit button by default. Change the Label in the Properties inspector to Submit Form.

Figure 9.20: Submit button properties

Add another button in the next column. Change the properties to look like this:

Figure 9.21: Reset button properties

The Submit button doesn't do anything at the moment; we'll cover that later.

Your form should look something like the one below:

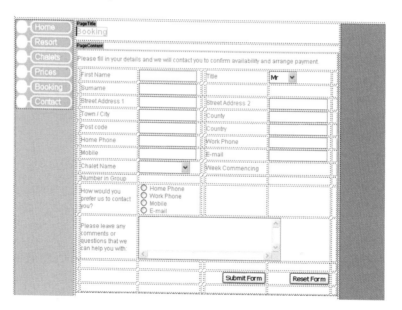

Figure 9.22

Save and preview your form.

Another way of adjusting column widths

You have probably already noticed that adjusting column widths in large tables by clicking and dragging table borders can be quite frustrating because Dreamweaver just doesn't seem to do what it's asked. The other way to do this is just to enter column widths in the Properties inspector.

▶   Click in a cell in the column you want to adjust, then enter a value in the W field in the Properties inspector. This will adjust the width of the whole column, not just that cell. In the screenshot above, a width of about 120 pixels was used for each of the 4 main columns, and 10 pixels for the 3 small columns. Change the table widths to pixels if they are currently in percent.

ℹ   This method doesn't work so well if there are a lot of merged cells in a table, such as the table on the Prices page.

Submitting the form

At the moment, clicking the Submit button will do nothing. To get this working, we will need to add code that will send the script (containing all the information entered by the user) to a specified e-mail address. This is actually much easier than it sounds – all you have to do is add a couple of entries in the Properties inspector.

▶   Click in one of the cells in the form.

▶   Select the whole form by clicking the <form> tag in the Tag selector. The whole form should be shaded grey to show that it is selected.

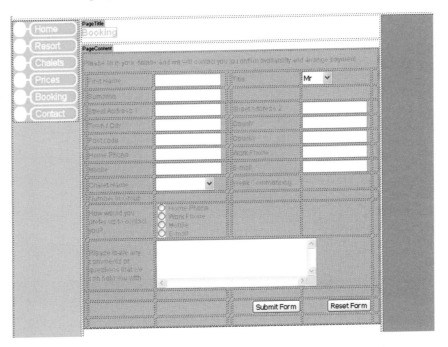

Figure 9.23: Selecting the whole form

- In the Properties inspector, name the form BookingForm by entering this in the FormName box.

- In the Action field, enter mailto:youremail@home.com, substituting your e-mail address where it says youremail@home.com. You must enter a valid e-mail address or you won't be able to test it properly.

- Enter the other details as shown in the screenshot below.

Figure 9.24: Form properties

- Save the Booking page then preview it in a browser.

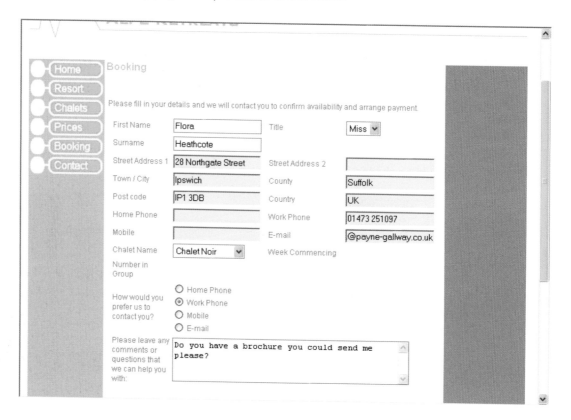

Figure 9-25: Previewing the form in Internet Explorer

Note: The fields may appear yellow in your browser.

● You can test the form even though your site isn't on a server yet. If you are online, preview the form and click the Submit button.

Figure 9.26: Your browser may generate this message about sending e-mails

Tip: This won't work if you're not online. Also, you need to make sure you have an e-mail client set up. If you're not sure, go to **Internet Explorer**, then select **Tools**, **Internet Options**. Click the **Programs** tab and make sure there is a program selected for e-mail. If not, choose something like **Outlook Express** if you have it.

● Click Yes to the prompt about whether or not you want to send an e-mail.

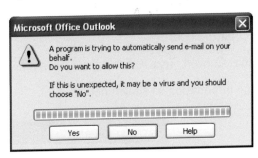

Figure 9.27: Outlook Express may generate this message about sending e-mails

● Click Yes (Send in version MX). You may get slightly different messages depending on which browser and e-mail client you are using.

Tip: If you cannot get this to work, it's possible that it is because of the e-mail settings on your computer, not the settings on the web page. Try sending the form from a different computer or changing the address the form is sent to.

● Check your inbox to see if it worked! If it doesn't work, go back to the Booking form in Dreamweaver and check the settings in the Property inspector.

Tip: If you send the form to a hotmail account it might end up in your Junk Mail folder – remember to look there if it doesn't appear in your inbox!

● You may find that the form posts a blank e-mail with an attachment called POSTDATA.ATT. If so, save the attachment then open it in a word package such as Notepad or MS Word.

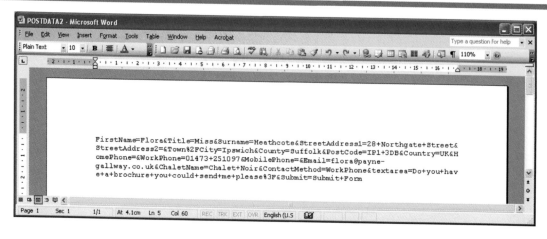

Figure 9.28: This is the e-mail attachment POSTDATA.ATT opened in Word

This looks a bit scrambled, but all the information from the form is here.

Formatting the data

To get this data looking more readable, you can put it into a table easily in Word.

- ◉ First select all the text.
- ◉ Select Table, Convert, Text to Table from the menu bar in Word.
- ◉ Fill out the information as shown below:

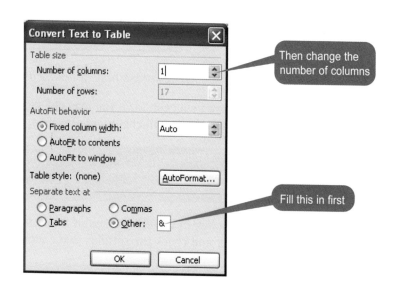

Figure 9.29: Converting text to table

⊙   Click OK. The data is now in a table!

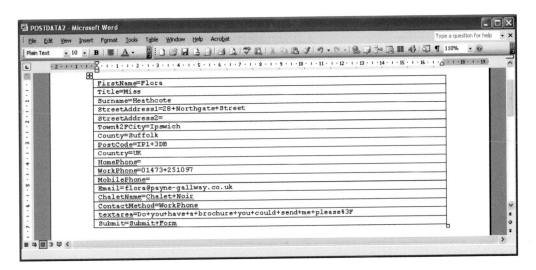

Figure 9.30

⊙   In Dreamweaver, save and close the Booking form.

The Contact page

The contact page is a simple table with addresses, phone numbers and an e-mail address for Alpe Retreats.

⊙   Create a new page based on the template, and save it as Contact.html.

⊙   Insert the table then enter the text as shown in Figure 9.31.

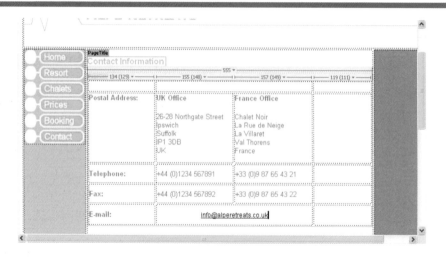

Figure 9.31: The Contact page

Tip: Pressing **Enter** after each line of the address gives a larger gap than you really want. To make text go onto another line without starting a new paragraph, hold down the **Shift** key then press **Enter**.

> ○ Use the Email Link icon on the Insert bar to add the e-mail link.

> ○ Save the page. Preview the page then close it.

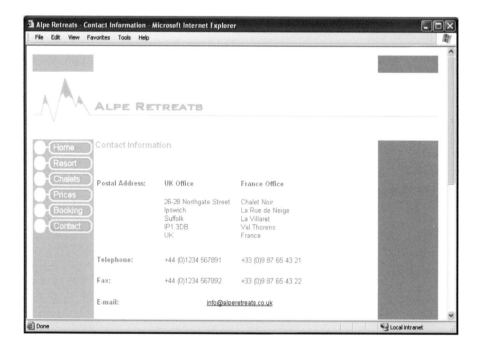

Figure 9.32: Previewing the Contact page

Finishing off

You've now created all the pages in the website. Now you need to make sure that all the buttons on the nav bar are linked to the correct pages (you'll need to do this in the template). Preview the site in a browser and check all the links. It is possible that pages will appear slightly differently in a browser to how they appear in Design view; if this is the case change the page in Design view so that it looks correct in the browser.

▶   When you're happy that the whole site works as it should, save and close all the pages.

Tip: Remember to save all the pages before previewing them in a browser. If you don't save, the page might not update and the browser won't reflect the most recent changes.

You've now created a website! Next we'll focus on how to get your website online. Don't worry if you don't have any web space at the moment – the next chapter will suggest how to get some free.

▶   Reopen the template file and make sure all the nav bar buttons go to the relevant pages (refer to Figure 7.11 if you need help).

▶   Save and close the template.

Getting your Website Online

10

You've created a website but at the moment you can only see it on your computer. This chapter explains how to make your website accessible to anyone on the Internet.

You can view your website on your own computer because all the files that make up your website are stored on your computer. In order that everyone can see your website, you need to transfer these files onto the server of your Web Host.

The method of transferring files that we will use is called File Transfer Protocol or FTP. Sounds scary – but really it isn't. If you are unsure of what you're doing, just follow the instructions below and you should be OK!

> **Tip:** You don't need to download any other FTP software, Dreamweaver is the FTP software (or FTP client) we will be using.

There are three steps to this, which I will cover in more detail in a minute:

- The first step is to make sure that you have access to some web space. If you don't already have some you can sign up for some free web space.

- The second step is to list key pieces of information about your web host account (things like server address – we'll go through this later). You will need this information to enter into Dreamweaver so that when it tries to connect to your web host server it knows where the server is and where your personal directory is on that server.

- The final step is to enter these pieces of information into Dreamweaver. This is really straightforward – you literally just type it in.

If you already have web space

If you already have access to some web space and want to use it for your website the first thing to do is to find out key information from your web host. To make things easier, the information needed for some popular web host companies (some of which are also ISPs – Internet Service Providers) is listed on the Payne-Gallway website.

- Go to www.payne-gallway.co.uk/dreamweaver and see if your web host is listed in the ISP information resource file. Note down the information relevant to your web host. There are also other tips on the website for you to follow if your web host isn't listed.

Signing up for free web space

There are several companies that provide free web space. Any site offering free web hosting will give you on-screen instructions on how to set up the account from their home page. we'll go through how to set up a Portland account as an example.

> **Tip:** If you go to **http://www.thefreecountry.com/webhosting/index.shtml** there is an up-to-date list of companies that provide free web hosting.

◉ Go to www.portland.co.uk.

Figure 10.1: The Portland website

◉ Select Free Web Hosting. This front page may be updated regularly so don't worry if yours looks a bit different. Just look for a link to Free Web Hosting.

◉ Follow the next link to Free Web Hosting.

◉ Click on the last link if you don't have a domain name.

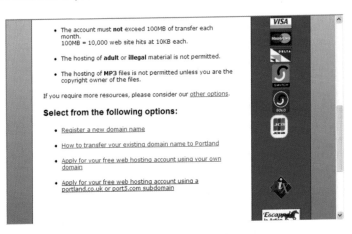

Figure 10.2: The Portland website

○ Now fill out the form. Remember your SubDomain Name – you'll need this later. Click Submit.

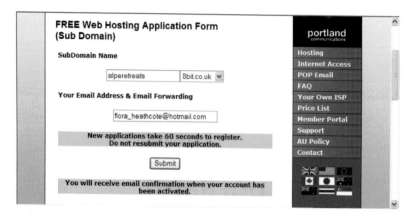

Figure 10.3: The Portland website

○ All done! Now check your e-mail for confirmation that the account has been set up. You will need this e-mail because it contains your user ID and password.

Figure 10.4: The Portland website

Tip: It can sometimes take a while for the e-mail to arrive so don't worry if it isn't there straightaway.

Your website address will be something like (but not the same as):

http://alperetreats.8bit.com

Now you need to transfer the web page files to the Portland (or other) web server. We'll use Dreamweaver to FTP the files over.

Setting up the Remote Info in Dreamweaver

◐ Open Dreamweaver. Select Site, Manage Sites from the menu (Edit Sites in version MX).

◐ Select Alpe Retreats then click Edit. Under the Advanced tab click Remote Info in the left-hand list.

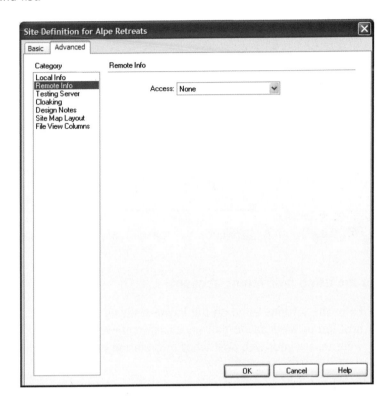

Figure 10.5: Setting up the Remote Info in the Site Definition window

If you have just signed up for a Portland account

◐ If you have just signed up with Portland, enter the following settings into Dreamweaver:

Access: FTP

FTP Host: ftp.portland.co.uk

Host Directory: (leave blank)

Login: your User ID – Portland will have e-mailed this to you

Password: your Password – Portland will have e-mailed this to you

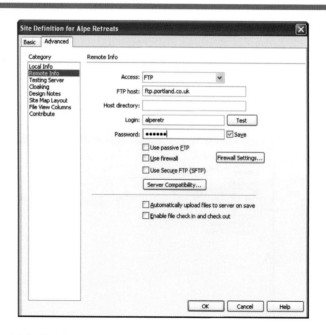

Figure 10.6: Setting up the Remote Info in the Site Definition window

If you are using a different account

○ Enter the settings listed on the Payne-Gallway website that are relevant to your web host (go to www.payne-gallway.co.uk/dreamweaver). If your web host is not listed on the website, ask your web host what information needs to be entered into the FTP client.

Does it work?

○ When you have entered all the information, click the Test button next to the Login field.

Figure 10.7

Figure 10.8

If this shows an error, you will need to go back and check all the information you entered. Sometimes if the server is busy it will look like it hasn't worked when really all the information is correct – click the test button a few times just to make sure this isn't the case.

◉   If it has worked you'll get a message saying Connected to Server.

Figure 10.9: Connecting to the remote server

◉   When it looks like it's working, click OK. Click OK in the Site Definition window then Done in the Manage Sites window.

Cloaking

Before transferring all the files to the server, you need to mark some files that don't need to be transferred. This is called Cloaking. The templates folder doesn't need to be transferred so we'll cloak this now.

◉   First, select Site, Manage Sites from the menu. Select Alpe Retreats then click Edit.

◉   Select Cloaking in the Category list on the left.

◉   Click the Enable Cloaking checkbox.

Figure 10.10: Enabling cloaking

◉   Click OK, then click Done in the Manage Sites window.

▶ Now, in the Files panel right-click the Templates folder.

Figure 10.11: Cloaking

▶ Select Cloaking, Cloak from the context menu.

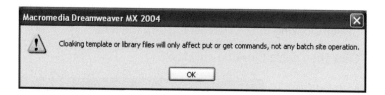

Figure 10.12: Cloaking

▶ Click OK to the message that appears. Notice that the Templates folder now has a red line through it.

Figure 10.13: Cloaking

▶ Cloak the Library folder in the same way.

Transferring the files

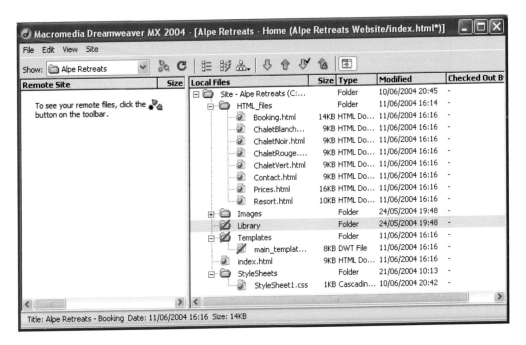

In the Files panel, click the Expand/Collapse icon.

Figure 10.14: The Files panel expanded

Tip: Many web hosts automatically create a file called **index.html** which will appear in the left-hand window. When you transfer your files across, your **index.html** file will overwrite this.

Connecting to the remote host

The remote host is the server that is providing the web space (e.g. Portland).

Click the Connect to Remote Host icon in the Files panel.

When connected, you should now see your root directory in the left-hand window. Portland has automatically created a folder into which all your files and folders need to go.

Get and Put

Loading files onto the server and removing them is called Get and Put. You need to Put all the files (apart from those you have cloaked) onto the server now.

You can use the Get and Put icons in the Files panel. But you may prefer to just click and drag the files across.

Click the index.html file on the right of the screen, and drag it across to the left-hand window. Drop it in the root directory (the top folder).

○   You are asked if you want to transfer Dependent files. Click Yes to this – the dependent files needed are basically the image files, but can also include other coding etc. It is safest to include them so you can be sure you have all the required files on the server.

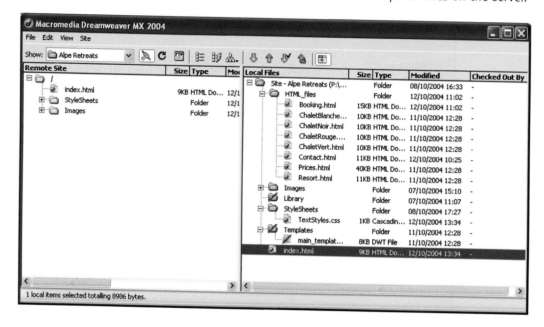

Figure 10.15: The Files panel expanded

Notice that the Images and StyleSheets folders have also been transferred – this is because they contain files that are used on the index.html page. If you expand the Images folder you'll see that it only contains the images that are used on the index.html page.

Now we'll transfer all the other files in one go.

○   Click the Images folder, hold down the Ctrl key then click the HTML_files folder. Both folders should now be selected.

○   Click and hold somewhere in the selection and drag all the files across to the left-hand window. Drop them in the top folder. Click Yes to include Dependent files.

These files may take a while to upload. When it's done, the files should appear on the left-hand part of the screen. That means that they're on the server.

Your website is now officially online!

○   If you are still connected to the server, click the Disconnect icon.

Viewing the website on the Internet

If you are with Portland, your website address will be:

http://sitename.port5.com (your sitename will be different)

Your individual web address will be in the e-mail sent to you by Portland.

> **Tip:** If you are connected to the server and don't do anything on it for a while, the connection may time-out. If this happens, just reconnect by clicking the **Connect** icon.

○ Open up a browser window and type the address above, substituting your own site name.

Figure 10.16: Viewing your site online

There it is! Don't worry if your site is not there immediately; some servers will take up to 48 hours to show your website for the first time (updates won't take this long).

> **Tip:** It is important that you type in **http://sitename.port5.com**, rather than **www.sitename.port5.com**. It won't work otherwise!

Testing

It is essential to check that all the pages appear as you expect them to.

○ Browse through the site, just as you would expect a potential customer to do.

Editing pages and uploading them

Making the changes offline

○   Open the page you want to edit. You must open the file that is on your computer (i.e. on the right-hand window when you expand the Files panel, not the file that is on the server).

○   Save the changes you made.

Uploading the updated pages onto the server

Now you need to Put the file onto the server. This file will overwrite the existing file on the server.

○   Expand the Files panel. Connect to the server so that you can see all the online files in the left-hand window. Click and drag the updated file from the right of the screen and drop it onto the existing file of the same name in the left of the window.

○   Click Yes to the prompt about overwriting the existing file. The updated file is now on the server – view it online to check that the changes have been made.

Updating the website online

If you like, you can connect to the server and open a page that is on the server by double-clicking it in the left-hand pane of the expanded Files panel.

By updating a page on the server, you will no longer have the most up-to-date version of the site on your own computer. It's recommended that you keep an up-to-date copy of the site, so that you are not dependent on the server should there be a problem at their end.

Updating the Prices page

The Prices page contains information about the number of places left in each chalet. This means that the Prices page must be regularly updated as the places are taken. To update a page like this you would follow the steps given above – basically make the changes then reload the file back onto the server; the old file will be overwritten by the updated file.

Frames

Frames are a slightly different way of designing a website. They can be very useful but they can also cause problems for older browsers and for search engines; for these reasons many web designers choose not to use them.

We'll cover frames briefly so that you know what they are and how to use them.

We'll create a couple of pages from the Alpe Retreats website using frames – you can go on to complete the whole site if you like.

What are frames?

Basically, frames divide up the browser window into more than one section, and each section displays a different web page. While the user will have gone to one web address, and think they are viewing one web page, they are actually viewing two or more pages. Each section is called a frame, and the collection of frames is called a frameset.

Why is this useful?

A particularly good use of frames is to display the contents or index of a site in one frame, while displaying the currently selected index item in another frame. In the Alpe Retreats website, we've used a nav bar and a template to ensure the site contents were always visible and each page looked similar; with frames, the nav bar would be a page of its own displayed in a frame, and whatever the user was looking at would be displayed in another frame. Additionally, the Alpe Retreats logo would be on its own on a page, displayed in its own frame.

Creating a new website

○ Using either Windows Explorer or the Files panel in Dreamweaver, create a new folder in the same place as you created the Alpe Retreats Website folder. Name the new folder Alpe Retreats using frames.

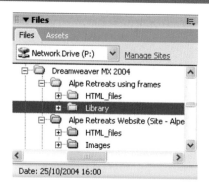

Figure 11.1

◉ Create the folders shown above.

◉ Copy and paste the Images folder and the StyleSheets folder from the original Alpe Retreats site to the new Alpe Retreats using frames site.

> **Tip:** To copy and paste a folder, go to Windows Explorer, select the folder you want to copy by clicking it once, then select **Copy** from the **Edit** menu. Now select the folder you want the other folder to be in and select **Edit, Paste**.

◉ In Dreamweaver, select Site, Manage Sites from the main menu bar. In the Manage Sites window select New, then Site from the menu that appears.

◉ Click the Advanced tab.

◉ Name the site AlpeRetreats_frames.

◉ Click the Browse icon next to the Local Root Folder field and find the Alpe Retreats using frames folder you have just created.

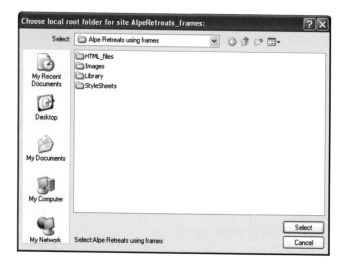

Figure 11.2: Choosing a local root folder

Your site definition should look like Figure 11.3.

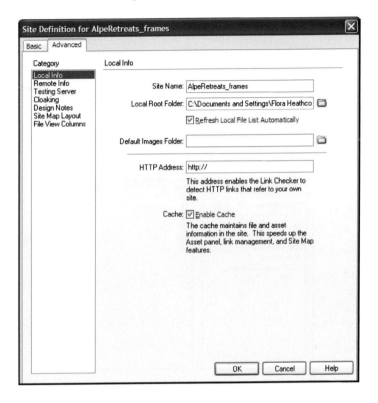

Figure 11.3: The Site Definition window

Note: The Local Root Folder address will depend on where you have put the site.

- Check that the details are correct, click OK, then Done.
- If it is not already selected, select AlpeRetreats_frames from the drop-down list at the top of the Files panel.

Creating frames

First we will create the Frameset: that is, create a new page and divide it into frames. Next we will insert the nav bar and the Alpe Retreats title graphic into their relevant frames. The pages of the website that will change as the user goes through the site (the Home page, Resort page etc) will be created separately, then the links will be added to display these pages in a frame. Don't worry about understanding all this – you'll see what happens when you work through the chapter.

Creating the Frameset

Now we'll create a page, divide it into frames then specify which page will appear in each frame.

▶   In Dreamweaver, open a new page by selecting File, New from the menu. Under the General tab, select Basic Page in the Category list and HTML in the right-hand list. Click Create.

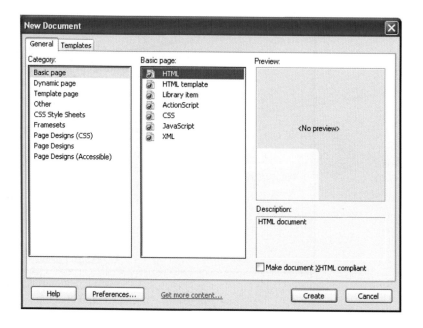

Figure 11.4: Creating a new page

Note: In version MX a blank page is automatically created when you open Dreamweaver so you don't need to create another one.

▶   Select the Layout tab on the Insert bar.

Figure 11.5: The Layout tab

 ▶   Find the frameset shown (Top and Nested Left Frames) from the Frames dropdown menu and select it.

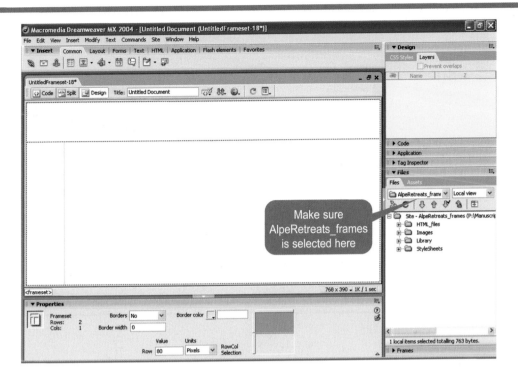

Figure 11.6

Your screen is divided into three frames.

ℹ You can actually get a huge combination of frame patterns by clicking in one of the frames and further dividing it into more frames by clicking another frameset icon. Experiment with this if you like – just select Edit, Undo from the menu when you're done to leave the page looking like the one above.

An alternative method

You can create the same frameset by a different method:

◉ Select File, New from the menu.

◉ Select Framesets from the left-hand list, and Fixed Top, Nested Left from the right-hand list.

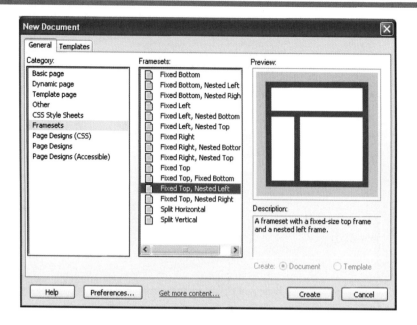

Figure 11.7

◗ Click **Create**. You'll have to delete one of the framesets if you now have two – you only need one.

The Frames panel

◗ Make sure you can see the **Frames** panel. In version MX it appears in the **Advanced Layout** panel group; in version MX 2004 it is not in a panel group, it sits alone. Either way, if it is not visible, select **Window**, **Frames** from the menu.

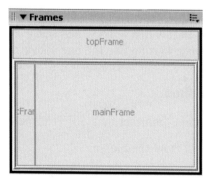

Figure 11.8: The Frames panel

Note: In version MX, click the **Frames** tab on the **Advanced Layout** panel group.

- Click in the topFrame.

- Rename it in the Properties inspector as titleFrame. Click Enter and the name should change in the Frames panel.

Figure 11.9: Frame properties

- Name the other two frames in the same way as navbarFrame and changingFrame.

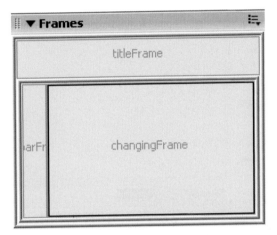

Figure 11.10: The Frames panel

Tip: If the name of the frames doesn't update in the **Frames** panel, it is probably because you didn't press **Enter** after renaming the frame.

Saving the Frameset

The collection of three frames is called a frameset. You have to save the frameset separately from the individual frames.

◉   Select File, Save Frameset from the main menu bar.

◉   Enter index.html as the file name then save it in the root directory (the Alpe Retreats using Frames directory) and click Save.

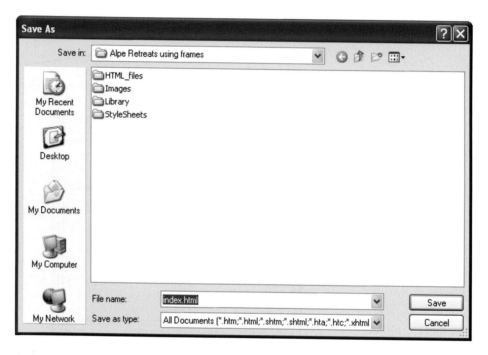

Figure 11.11: Saving the Frameset

Saving the frames

As well as saving the Frameset, you have to save each of the three frames.

◉   Select the titleFrame by clicking it in the main window (not by using the Frames panel).

◉   Select File, Save Frame from the main menu bar.

◉   Enter title_frame.html then save it in the HTML_files folder.

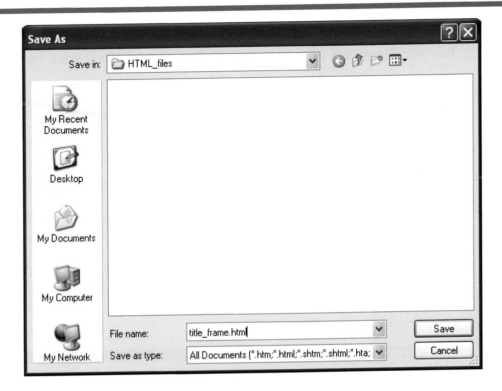

Figure 11.12: Saving the title frame

○ Save the other frames as navbar_frame.html and changing_frame.html.

Is everything saved?

It can get quite confusing when using frames because you have to name frames, and save them, and then save the frameset! And to make matters worse, if you haven't saved everything you will get error messages when you try and preview the page. One of the simplest ways of making sure everything is saved before previewing a site is to Save All.

○ Right-click on the page tab of the frameset and select Save All from the shortcut menu that appears.

The nav bar

First we'll design the frame that contains the nav bar: this will go in the left-hand frame.

- ◉ Click in the navbarFrame.

- ◉ First create a table with 3 rows and 1 column. Once the table is created, convert the width to pixels.

 ◉ Next, create a nav bar in the centre row of the table you just created.

The nav bar will be exactly the same as you created in Chapter 3 for the original Alpe Retreats website in the template. Be sure to use the images from the correct folder – remember you've got an identical Images folder in both the original and new Alpe Retreats sites. Leave the When Clicked fields blank for now.

Make sure you select the Use Tables and Insert Vertically options.

- ◉ Stretch the table vertically so that it covers at least the length of the window. Click and drag the frame border to fit the width of the nav bar. Colour the table background to match the grey in the nav bar.

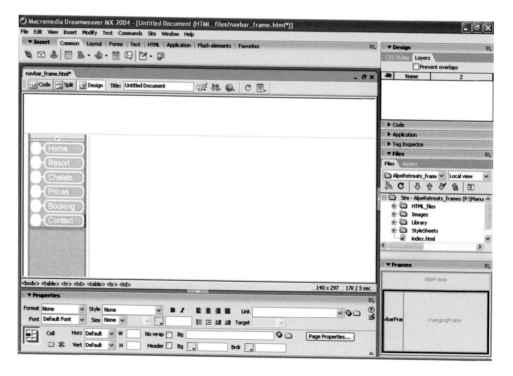

Figure 11.13

The title frame

Now we'll create the web page containing the title; this will go in the titleFrame.

▶ Click in the titleFrame.

▶ Insert the image AlpeRetreats_logo.jpg.

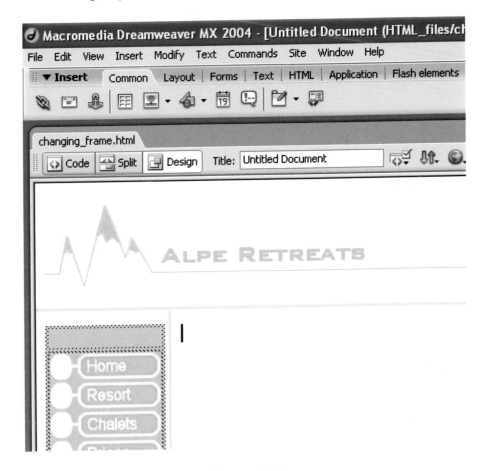

Figure 11.14

▶ Click and drag the frame borders to resize the frames if you need to. You will probably find that you want to scroll around a frame but that there are no scroll bars – use the arrow keys on your keyboard instead.

▶ Save All and close the frameset for now.

Creating the Home page

The Home page will appear in the changingFrame. The contents of this frame will change between displaying the Home page, the Resort page and the other pages in the site according to what the user has selected on the nav bar.

- Select File, New to create a new blank page.

- Select Basic Page from in the Category list and HTML from the right-hand list. Click Create.

- Create the home page in just the same way as you did in the original site (except with no template) so that it looks like the page below.

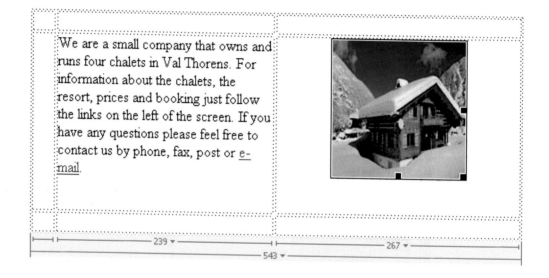

Figure 11.15: The home page

- Save the page but don't close it.

Importing CSS Styles

Since we've already created the styles we need when we created the other website we really want to reuse them.

> **Note**: When we set up the frames site we copied across the **StyleSheets** folder. This wasn't absolutely necessary because you can attach a style sheet that is not stored as a file within a particular site; you could, for example just attach the style sheet from the other site. The reason for having a copy is simply in case you want to store the frames site on a different computer from the original site.

 ◗ Open and expand the CSS Styles panel. At the bottom of the panel, click the Attach Style Sheet icon.

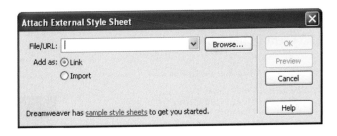

Figure 11.16: Attaching a style sheet

◗ Click the Browse button. In the Select Style Sheet File window find the TextStyles.css file in the StyleSheets folder. Make sure you select the folder that is under the Alpe Retreats using Frames folder.

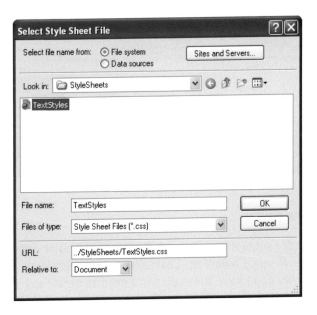

Figure 11.17: Attaching a style sheet

●   Click OK. Click OK again in the **Attach External Style Sheet** window.

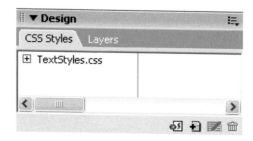

Figure 11.18: The CSS Styles panel

The **TextStyles** style sheet appears in the **CSS Styles** panel.

●   Apply the **PageContent** style to the text by highlighting the text then selecting **PageContent** in the **Properties** inspector.

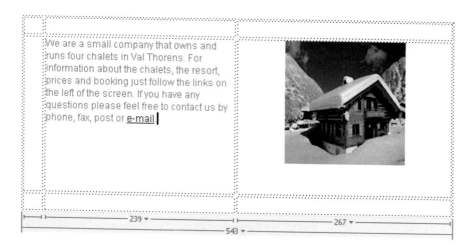

Figure 11.19

Note: If you were creating more than one web page you could set up one folder for all your favourite CSS Styles and use the same style sheet for all the web page. In each new site just attach the style sheet using the **Attach Style Sheet** icon in the **CSS Styles** panel.

Creating the other pages

Now create the other pages in the website just as you've done the Home page — there should be pages for **Resort**, **ChaletVert**, **ChaletBlanche**, **ChaletRouge**, **ChaletNoir**, **Prices**, **Booking** and **Contact**. If you don't have time you don't need to create every page, but you should create the Resort page and at least one of the Chalet pages to use later on.

●   Save all the pages and close them.

Selecting the source of each frame

Now you need to specify a source for the changingFrame. Although the contents of this frame will change when the user selects an option from the nav bar, the source you select here is the one that will first appear when a user logs on to your site.

○ Open the index.html file. If you can't see the frame borders select View, Visual Aids, Frame Borders from the menu bar.

○ Click in the changingFrame in the Frames panel.

○ Make sure the home.html file is visible in the Files panel.

 ○ Drag the target icon from the Src field in the Properties inspector and drop it on the home.html file in the Files panel.

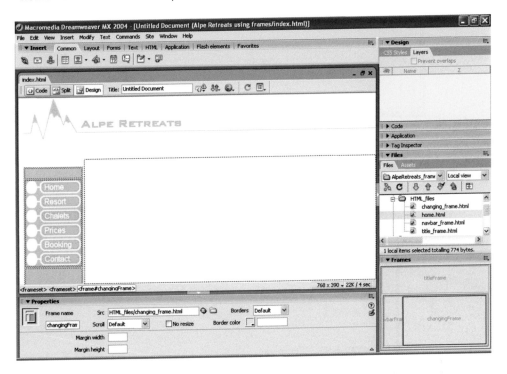

Figure 11.20: Selecting a source for the changingFrame

The home.html page now appears in the main frame!

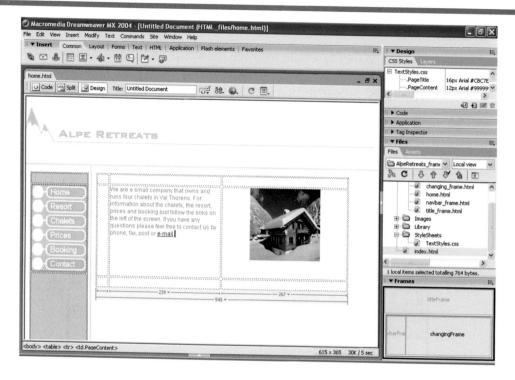

Figure 11.21

⊙   Save the frameset then preview the page in a browser.

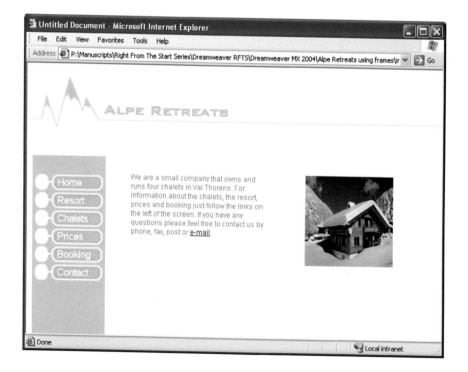

Figure 11.22: Previewing the Frameset

The Chalet Submenu

You can use layers with frames, but in our case the submenu layer cannot sit in the same position because it would be overlapping with the changing Frame. For the layer to work it would have to be entirely in the navbarFrame. I would suggest that you create an extra page called ChaletSubmenu.html that appears in the changingFrame when the Chalets navbar button is clicked. This page will contain links to each of the four chalet pages.

> **Tip:** To save time, open the template file **main_template.dwt** in the **Templates** folder of the original Alpe Retreats site. Go to the **Layers** panel and unhide the **Submenu** layer. Click in the layer and use the **<table>** tag to select the whole table then select **Edit**, **Copy** from the menu. On the new **ChaletSubmenu** page select **Edit**, **Paste**. Remember to change the hyperlinks to the new chalet pages, not the ones in the old site. Press **Enter** two or three times to add some blank lines above the table.

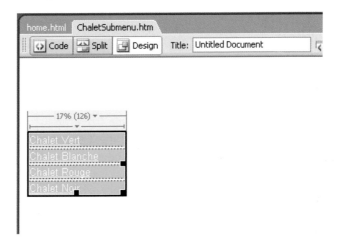

Figure 11.23: The ChaletSubmenu page

Creating hyperlinks to open in the changingFrame

◉   Click the Resort button on the nav bar.

◉   Now click on the <a> tag at the bottom of the screen so that the button is greyed-out.

Figure 11.24: Selecting the Resort button

 In the **Properties** inspector, drag the target icon next to the **Link** field onto the **Resort.html** file in the **Files** panel.

In the **Target** field, select **changingFrame** from the list. This means that the **Resort** page will open in the **changingFrame**. If you don't specify a target, the page would open in the same frame as the **Resort** button, i.e. the **navbarFrame**.

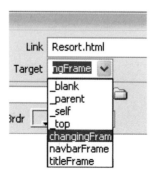

Figure 11.25: Selecting a Target for the link

Repeat this for the chalet button, which will link to the **ChaletSubmenu**. You will still need to make a hyperlink for the **Home** button so that you can return to the home page after viewing other pages.

Save all the frames and the frameset then preview the site in a browser.

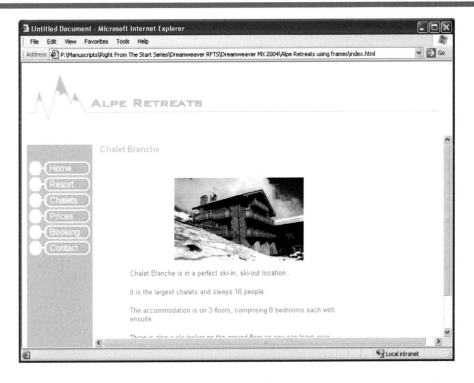

Figure 11.26: Previewing the final site in a browser

The site will feel quite similar to the original site. One of the user-friendly things about using frames is that the title bar and nav bar don't move – in the original site if you scroll down or across a page you can easily lose sight of the title and nav bar.

That's it!

Index

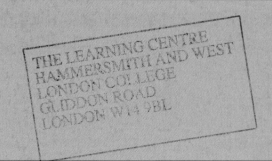